An Open Letter to

ALL

Regarding Donald Sterling

Bryant T. Jordan

Sports Seer Publishing

An Open Letter to ALL Regarding Donald Sterling

Published by Sports Seer Publishing

Library and Archives Canada Cataloguing in Publication

Jordan, Bryant T., 1979-, author

An open letter to everyone regarding Donald Sterling / Bryant T. Jordan.

Issued in print and electronic formats.

ISBN 978-1-927654-29-3 (pbk.).--ISBN 978-1-927654-30-9 (bound).--

ISBN 978-1-927654-31-6 (pdf)

1. Sterling, Donald, 1934-. 2. Racism. 3. National Basketball Association.

4. Los Angeles Clippers (Basketball team). 5. Basketball team owners--California--

Los Angeles. I. Title.

GV884.S74J67 2014 796.323092 C2014-903541-1

C2014-903542-X

Publisher: **www.SportsSeerPublishing.com**

First Book: **www.SavingTheLakers.com**

Second Book: **www.SavingTheCeltics.com**

Author: **www.BryantTJordan.com**

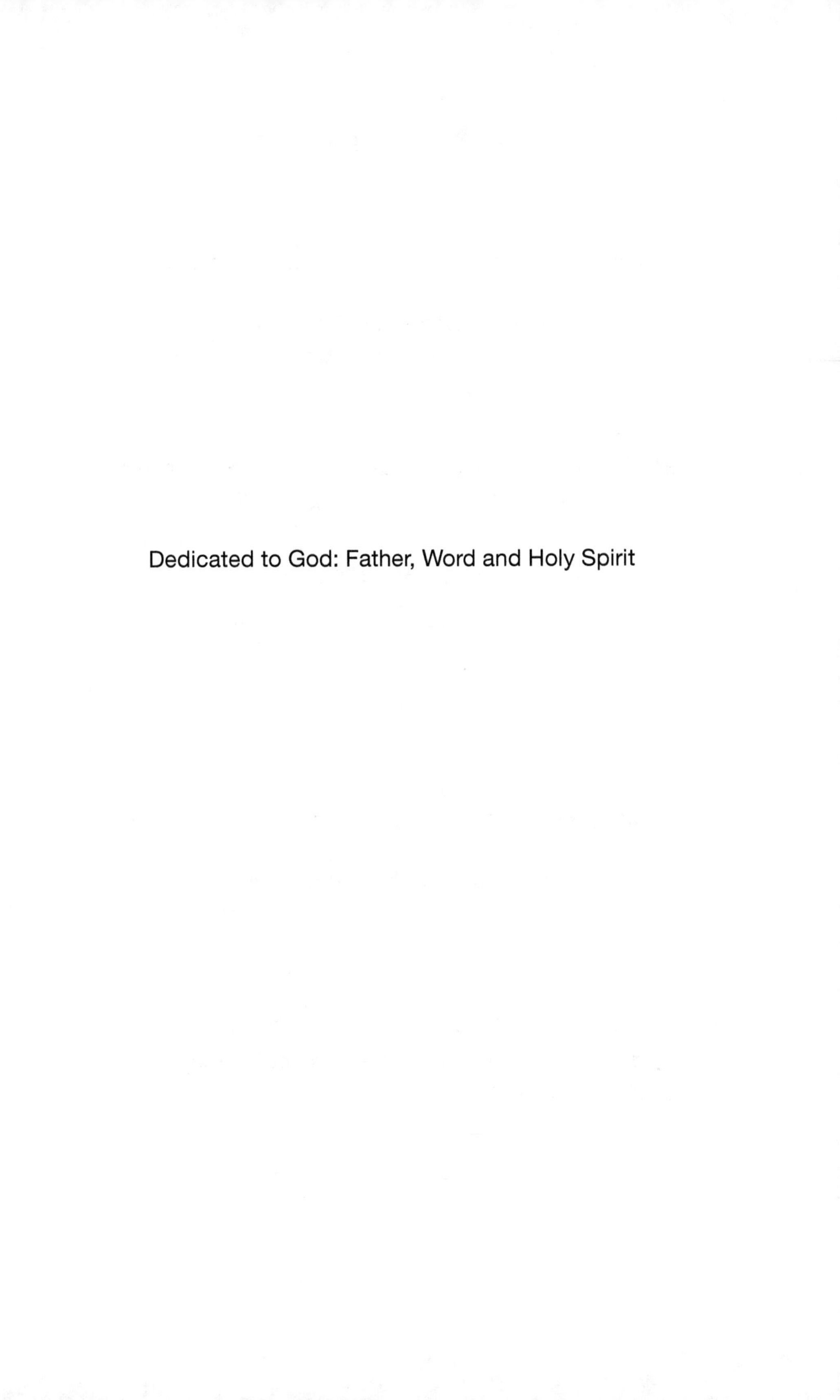

Dedicated to God: Father, Word and Holy Spirit

Also by Bryant T. Jordan:

Saving the Lakers: A Be the General Manager Book

www.SavingTheLakers.com

Bryant T. Jordan's Saving the Lakers is a stats-geek and moneyballers dream! This book rocks!

- Paula Vincent, Reader

Saving the Celtics: A Be the General Manager Book

www.SavingTheCeltics.com

I don't even like the Celtics and yet I love this book.
It's like a VIDEO-GAME ON PAPER, this book rocks!
Read this book and give a copy to all your buddies.

- Noah Jefferson, Reader

I don't want you to have hate. That's what people do they turn things around... Which are all lies. I love the black people... I love everybody.

-Donald Sterling

For if ye forgive men their trespasses, your heavenly Father will also forgive you: But if ye forgive not men their trespasses, neither will your Father forgive your trespasses.

- Jesus Christ of Nazareth

Ye have heard that it hath been said, Thou shalt love thy neighbour, and hate thine enemy. But I say unto you, Love your enemies, bless them that curse you, do good to them that hate you, and pray for them which despitefully use you, and persecute you; That ye may be the children of your Father which is in heaven: for he maketh his sun to rise on the evil and on the good, and sendeth rain on the just and on the unjust. For if ye love them which love you, what reward have ye? do not even the publicans the same? And if ye salute your brethren only, what do ye more than others? do not even the publicans so? Be ye therefore perfect, even as your Father which is in heaven is perfect.

- Jesus Christ of Nazareth

A woman always remembers; remember that.

-Magic Johnson

ACKNOWLEDGEMENTS

First and foremost I want to thank my first love, God the Father, Word and Holy Spirit. Without Him I am nothing.

I would also like to thank my Grandmother. You taught me to think for myself, to be true to myself, and to follow my heart no matter what anyone else thought. I sincerely thank you for that.

Last but certainly not least I would like to thank my magnificent wife and our precious children; words cannot express how thankful I am to have been blessed with each and every one of you and how very much I love you. May you each serve God above all and always do what you believe is right, no matter what anyone else thinks, says, or does!

CONTENTS

Prologue 11

Open Letter to ALL Regarding Donald Sterling 17

Epilogue 63

Complete Transcript of the Sterling Recordings 71

Complete Transcript of Adam Silver's News Conference 83

Suggested Reading 93

BONUS: Prologue from *Saving the Lakers: A Be the General Manager Book* 97

BONUS: Introduction from *Saving the Celtics: A Be the General Manager Book* 105

About the Author 111

PROLOGUE

I remember the first time I ever met a black person in-person, or perhaps I should say, I remember the first time I ever met a black person I remember meeting in-person. Her name was Tara Weston and she took my breath away.

I had just moved to the city with my mom after she left my country bumpkin dad (I say this in love as I adore that country bumpkin) to play the field and take a higher paying job when I was 8 years old. I had seen a few black people on television growing up, namely the *Huxtables* and the *Jeffersons* as well as some athletes. However, since we only owned a television for perhaps a total of ten months out of my first eleven years of life, I can't really remember seeing any other black people, even on television, other than athletes. Dominique Wilkins was my favorite athlete, followed by Charles Barkley, Isaih Thomas and Dennis Rodman.

From just about the first moment I laid eyes on Tara, I must have unconsciously determined that black women were more attractive than white women, period. I say this because from the time I met Tara until the moment I meant my wife to be, upwards of ninety percent of the women I had crushes on or found extremely attractive were black. My wife (who is Caucasian and of French/English/German descent) often jokes, *I'm so happy you married me even though I was white.* There are no secrets between us and I often think she knows me better than I know myself.

To this day, if I had to create an NBA style 15 member team of the most *physically* attractive women of all time, my wife would be one of only four white women on the team, along with Raquel Welch, Monica Bellucci (whom my wife resembles) and Elle MacPherson. The remaining 11 members would be (in no particular order): Serena Williams, Vivica A. Fox, Beyonce Knowles, Paige Thomas (from season 2 of *X-Factor USA*), Kym Whitley, Nia Long, Cindy Herron, Onika Maraj (aka Nicki Minaj), Rosario Dawson, Paula Patton and Kim Kardashian. The team would be coached by Monica Potter, as if she can almost become Mayor of Berkeley (even if it was while playing *Kristina Braverman* on the best show on television, Parenthood) she could lead a team full of divas. Besides, I nearly fall in love with her every time I watch an old episode of *Boston Legal*.

However, I would make sure I also had Pam Grier, Adina Howard, Whitney Houston, Dana Owens (aka Queen Latifah), Tasha Smith, Deidra Roper (aka Spindarella), Jessica Alba, Jennifer Lopez, Vanessa Bryant (Kobe Bryant's wife), Brenda Song and Freida Pinto, as well as Caucasians Charlize Theron, Liv Tyler, Gemma Arterton and Cindy Crawford on my 15 member D-League affiliate. This team would be coached by Bridget Moynahan, as if she can handle herself in the New York District Attorney's Office (even if such only happens when she is acting as *Erin Reagan* in *Blue Bloods*) she could also lead a team full of divas. Besides, I also nearly fall in love with her every time I watch an episode of *Blue Bloods* as well, and personally I think Tom Brady was insane for choosing Gisele Bundchen over her!

Needless to say, I have no doubt my NBA and D-league teams would sell more tickets than any other teams in their respective sports. And, for the record, my star cheerleader would be Janet Jackson (I still remember watching the *Love will Never Do Without You* video on BET when I was 11 years old and just being blown away). And, the only announcer I would ever hire would be Jenifer Lewis, as in my mind, she has the greatest voice of all time, and it doesn't hurt that she is gorgeous as well.

For those keeping track at home, out of the 30 women on my two NBA style teams, 15 were black, eight were white, four were Latina, one was Armenian, one was Indian, one was Asian, and a great many would be considered of mixed ancestry. It would be next to impossible for me to rank these 30 women in any concrete way as the order would undoubtedly change constantly. However, I will say that my concrete Fabulous Four, in order, is:

1. My wife – seriously.
2. Serena Williams
3. Kym Whitley
4. Vivica A. Fox

I can also say that Monica Bellucci, Beyonce Knowles, Kim Kardashian and Paula Patton would be a lock for my Top 10 list no matter what day it was. Elle MacPherson, Rosario Dawson, Paige Thomas and Onika Maraj (aka Nicki Minaj) would fight it out for the tenth spot on most days.

Anyone reading this should be able to see the above lists are anything but sexist and that they are merely my honest opinion. Every woman on the planet is attractive in one way or another, and outside of the majority of my 15 member first team being black, there really is no defining physical characteristic each of the members on either team have. Just try to compare Kym Whitley with Cindy Herron or Rosario Dawson with Serena Williams or Monica Bellucci with Nia Long on the first team, or Dana Owens (aka Queen Latifah) with Freida Pinto or Tasha Smith with Brenda Song on the second team; such would be an exercise in futility to say the least!

In fact, compare my Top 30 list with the top 30 women listed on *FHM's 2014 Official 100 Sexiest Women in the World* where 27 of the top 30 are Caucasian and just two are black; two, now that is ridiculous!

I realize that Vivica A. Fox may no longer be the traffic stopping beauty she was in her 20s and that she's almost 50 years old now. But, she didn't even make the Top 100 while Caucasian Nigela Lawson, who *FHM* ranked #21 is 54 years old already! Something is just not right about that.

All of the above said and in all seriousness (I don't expect Vivica A. Fox to make it onto a list of the *Sexiest* women in the year 2014 at nearly 50 years old), the fact is that physical beauty is indeed found in all races, colors, shapes and sizes, and that beauty is indeed *in the eye of the beholder!* However, beauty is also *fleeting* and the most important characteristic any woman can truly have is that of a pure and beautiful spirit. That said, *God's Top 30* list could indeed be filled with woman that most men on this planet would not find *physically* attractive in any way, shape or form, and yet they would be the most beautiful of all!

Being a white kid originally from a small rural town, with only white relatives, some of whom were racist (though not my mom or dad) and enrolled in a High School that had a large contingent of self-proclaimed hicks from the sticks, the fact that I was primarily attracted to black classmates, had black friends, played hoops for probably a solid 25-35 hours per week, wore *Cross Colors* clothing, pimp walked and listened to 2PAC religiously, you can imagine I heard my fair share of *ni*g*r lover* and *wigger* (i.e. white ni*g*r) insults. However, such ignorant words never bothered me as I knew the people who spoke them were merely filled with hatred and in need of education and enlightenment.

I suppose my mom and dad deserve some credit as well, though I wouldn't have thought so at the time. My mom had left my dad and ended up dating multiple black men and almost marrying one of them (until he cheated on her – you reap what you sow). She even dated a man who had dated one of my classmates which grossed me out to no end. However, while I didn't approve of her leaving my dad, let alone of acting like a teenager and needing me to be the parent in the house, I most definitely did learn tolerance from her. As for my dad, he was a bumpkin, loved rock 'n' roll music, wore plaid shirts and tight jeans and loved Chuck Norris movies. However, he was also an extremely loving, caring and tolerant man who stood by his principles no matter what anyone else thought and was the type of man that would give a stranger the shirt of his back if necessary. When he was in High School back in the early '70s he took a black girl on a date and went for a stroll with her down by the boardwalk. A group of men saw him, jumped him and beat him so bad that he was hospitalized with broken ribs, though as my dad is quick to mention, not before he knocked a couple of them out and threw another one over the railing into the river below. Needless to say, I am my parents' child.

Even before I repented of my sins, believed on the Lord and Savior Jesus Christ of Nazareth and dedicated my life to my Creator, thereby understanding there was an actual divine reason to detest racism and an unchangeable code to live by that forbid racism of any kind, I simply couldn't wrap my mind around how anyone with a brain could hate, or even mildly dislike, someone else simply because of the color of his or her skin. Even though I was originally a boy from the sticks, such racist idiocy made no sense to me.

I did have racist relatives however, some of whom did not consider themselves racist, which basically sums up Donald Sterling in the minds of many. Now and then I would hear one of them tell a joke or make a racist remark and I would quickly jump down their throat and express my disgust with such. That didn't seem to stop them but at least they knew I disapproved.

However, perhaps I should have physically attacked the individuals who spoke such words, or cursed them and everyone associated with them (as Calvin Broadus, aka Snoop Dogg, aka Snoop Lion recently did to Donald Sterling), or keyed their car, or stole money out of their purse or wallet when they weren't looking? No, I don't think any of that would have been called for. Two wrongs don't make a right and rewarding evil with evil is never wise, period.

When someone uttered words that offended me I uttered words that let them know I was disgusted with their behavior. That seemed like an appropriate response to me then. I still feel the same way today.

> *That's just the way it is... I see no changes. All I see is racist faces. Misplaced hate makes disgrace to races, we under, I wonder what it takes to make this one better place? Let's erase the wasted. Take the evil out the people, they'll be acting right... And only time we chill is when we kill each other; it takes skill to be real, time to heal each other... Some things will never change.*
>
> *- Changes, Tupac Amaru Shakur aka 2PAC*

In *Changes,* Pac does not condemn racism as much as he admits it exists and challenges his listeners to remove the evil from themselves, act right and heal others. When the world heard Donald Sterling's voice on the infamous recordings released by TMZ and Deadspin, did they remove evil from their own heart, act right and try to heal Mr. Sterling and others? Or, did they reward evil with evil, act with their emotions rather than with reason and logic, and do anything but help try to heal Mr. Sterling or anyone else?

People can say whatever negative things they want about Tupac Shakur; I love him, respect him, consider him an artistic genius and happily credit him with contributing to my own dogged quest to remain true to myself no matter what anyone else thinks. Pac was a ghetto prophet as well as an enlightened soul; I truly believe that. He was also a tortured soul and someone who, like the Biblical Paul of Tarsus, could say, for what I would, that do I not; but what I hate, that do I (Romans 7: 15b). I can say the same. In fact, I think we all can, if we are honest with ourselves, whether our name is Donald Sterling, Barack Obama or any other name under the sun.

Martin Luther King, Jr. once wrote, while in jail for committing nonviolent civil disobedience during the Montgomery bus boycott:

> *We must develop and maintain the capacity to forgive. He who is devoid of the power to forgive is devoid of the power to love. There is some good in the worst of us and some evil in the best of us. When we discover this, we are less prone to hate our enemies. Forgiveness does not mean ignoring what has been done or putting a false label on an evil act. It means, rather, that the evil act no longer remains as a barrier to the relationship. Forgiveness is a catalyst creating the atmosphere necessary for a fresh start and a new beginning.*
>
> *- From The Class of Nonviolence, prepared by Colman McCarthy of the Center for Teaching Peace, 4501 Van Ness Street, NW, Washington, D.C. 20016 202/537-1372).*

Martin Luther King, Jr. was also a modern prophet, yet far too often his words are ignored by the very people he was trying to lead out of bondage (blacks with their bondage to oppression and unforgiveness and whites with their bondage to oppressing others and lack of true love for their fellow man), just as Moses words were ignored by the Israelites he lead out of Egypt, or Jesus' words were ignored by nearly everyone who heard Him. God sends the prophets to the earth and they are almost always rejected. This is to our shame.

MLK, like Tupac before him and Paul of Tarsus before him, knew that there is indeed good in the worst of us and evil in the best of us. I have no doubt that MLK would have advised his listeners to reprimand Donald Sterling for his offensive words with loving words of wisdom and rebuke, not with the maniacal insults, threats and hatred that Mr. Sterling ended up receiving.

There is good in Donald Sterling, of this I have no doubt. He has done a great deal more for a great many people than many of us would do for the same, and that isn't even debatable. Of course, there is also evil in Donald Sterling, and of this I also have no doubt. He has committed adultery which is a damnable sin for one (of course the NBA could care the less if one is committing a damnable sin, as such a sin is commonplace in the immoral age we find ourselves in and the NBA is concerned with money more so than morality). He is human, period. We all are.

MLK taught that when we realize there is *good in the worst of us and evil in the best of us* we are less prone to hate our enemies. I agree with him and can only assume that those individuals who lashed out at Donald Sterling did so because they are consumed with self-righteousness and feel there is no *evil* in their own heart. That or they are simply being hypocritical. Either way, such actions are to their shame.

MLK also taught that once one truly forgives, there will be no barrier to forming a relationship with the offending party and that a new beginning is possible for both parties. That is exactly what Tupac was teaching when he said, *Take the evil out the people, they'll be acting right... it takes skill to be real, time to heal each other.* Tupac was teaching people to look in the mirror and remove the evil from their own hearts, so that they could then start to heal others rather than merely compounding the problem and escalating the situation.

Martin Luther King and Tupac Shakur taught the same thing; crazy but true. The question is, will you listen to them, or is your hatred for Donald Sterling's supposed views and beliefs and therefore Donald Sterling himself, so great that you cannot forgive, cannot remove the *evil* from yourself, cannot act right and cannot *heal*?

If the latter is the case, please consider the words of Jesus Christ of Nazareth, the One who loved you enough to live a sinless yet thankless life on this earth, be tortured and ultimately crucified, and finally rise again to prove He had conquered death and hell, leaving you a perfect example to emulate and aspire too. For it was Jesus who said:

> *For if ye forgive men their trespasses, your heavenly Father will also forgive you: But if ye forgive not men their trespasses, neither will your Father forgive your trespasses.*

OPEN LETTER TO ALL REGARDING DONALD STERLING

If you haven't read the prologue, do so now. It is important. Thank you.

Donald Sterling. That name became perhaps the most popular name in America for a short time last April and May, for all the wrong reasons.

However, the entire Donald Sterling fiasco, like just about any other event, can teach all of us valid life lessons. And, in this particular case, we can all learn a great deal from Sterling's words as well as the NBA's and the public's reactions to such mere words.

> *Accordingly, effective immediately, I am banning Mr. Sterling for life from any association with the Clippers organization or the NBA. Mr. Sterling may not attend any NBA games or practices.*

> *He may not be present at any Clippers facility, and he may not participate in any business or player personnel decisions involving the team. He will also be barred from attending NBA Board of Governors meetings or participating in any other league activity. I am also fining Mr. Sterling $2.5 million, the maximum amount allowed under the NBA constitution.*

The above words were spoken by NBA Commissioner Adam Silver on April 29, 2014, just three days after Donald Sterling, one of the longest tenured owners in professional sports, turned 80 years old.

To someone like my 76 year old Grandmother, a lifelong public school teacher who helped raise me when my parents were acting the fool, who does not follow any sports, nor does she even read the newspaper or watch the news, anything other than once in a while, hearing Commissioner Silver's words on the eleven o'clock news set her mind to worrying. My Grandma has always been a worry-wart; she once called my wife and said, *Dear, if you are ever worried about anything, even if it's three in the morning, do call me, so I can worry with you; we'll worry together.* Yes, I'm serious; my Grandma cracks me up and could literally be one of the greatest stand-up comedians on the planet if someone would just give her a microphone and let her talk. She has almost no sense of humor, rarely understands any joke she hears and has no idea how to tell one (her idea of a joke is: *Knock, knock? ... Purple ... Purle Crown King*), yet she says some of the most off-the-wall hilarious things you could ever imagine.

Anyways, hearing that a man had been banned for life and fined such an incredibly large amount of money (modern NBA fans realize that $2.5 million is a pittance for a billionaire owner, but to a woman born in 1937 and who lived through the *Great Depression*, $2.5 million is an astronomical sum) set my Grandma to worrying something fierce. Her initial thoughts were that this Sterling fella must have killed someone, perhaps his wife. Maybe he had too much to drink and hit and killed a child crossing the road on a bicycle. Or, perhaps he is just one of those scoundrels who got caught stealing millions of dollars like that Bennie Magoo (i.e. Bernie Madoff) fella.

When I spoke with her on the phone she asked me about the *event* she recently heard about, what had actually happened and what I personally thought about it. When I explained to her that Donald Sterling was an 80 year old man, and that he had received the lifetime ban and large fine because a recording of a private conversation he had with his young mistress, which recorded him saying some politically-incorrect and racist things, had been made public, she was both confused and astounded.

My Grandmother simply could not understand how any individual could receive such a punishment for uttering private words. After quelling her fears that our own phone conversation was being tapped by *Big Brother* (my Grandmother is a George Orwell fan) and assuring her that she would not be arrested by the *Thought Police* or exiled to *Iceland* in this the year *106 A.F.* (i.e. After Ford – she is also a big Aldous Huxley fan) if she continued talking to me, she told me that the punishment Donald Sterling received for uttering mere words, scared her and that she didn't think it was *right* or *American*. Simply put, she didn't feel the punishment fit the crime.

Honestly, I had to agree with her because she was right. The punishment did not fit the crime, especially considering there was no *crime* to speak of. Uttering racist, sexist, immoral or unethical private words is not a crime, at least not in America.

On top of the fact that Donald Sterling did not commit any known crime, the simple fact is that even had he committed a *crime* with mere *words*, such as *slander,* the punishment he received would not fit such a *word-crime*. Not when one considers the following list of NBA players and executives who received little more than a slap on the wrist from the league:

> **Charles Smith:** Convicted of *vehicular homicide* after he hit and killed two Boston University students in 1991 while playing for the Boston Celtics. Just 3 years and 7 months after being convicted, the Philadelphia 76'ers signed him to a free agent contract and after releasing him, the Minnesota Timberwolves did the same.

Isiah Thomas: Lost a sexual harassment case and, along with *Madison Square* Garden, paid plaintiff Anucha Browne Sanders $11.5 million. Thomas is currently employed by NBA TV as a studio analyst.

Jason Kidd: Was charged with and pleaded *no contest* to spousal abuse. Was also charged with a DWI for an incident on July 15, 2012 when he smashed into a telephone pole. Kidd is currently employed by the NBA's Brooklyn Nets as head coach.

Joshua Richardson: Arrested for carrying a loaded handgun through airport security in Newark, New Jersey in 2012 while he was an Executive Director of the New Orleans Hornets. He is currently the Executive Director of Live Programming and Broadcasting for the NBA's New Orleans Pelicans.

Mike Budenholzer: Arrested on a DUI charge shortly after becoming the new head coach of the Atlanta Hawks in 2013. He is still the head coach of the Atlanta Hawks.

DeShawn Stevenson: Convicted of statutory rape of a 14 year old girl when he was 20 years of age. Stevenson currently plays for the NBA's Atlanta Hawks.

Ron Artest (aka Metta World Peace): Convicted for his part in the Palace of Auburn Hills brawl in which he ran into the stands and began assaulting a fan, for which he was suspended 72 games and the playoffs. Was also charged with and pleaded *no contest* to spousal abuse. Artest played for the NBA's New York Knicks last season. In fact, Artest is one of my own ten favorite players of All-Time along with Pete Maravich, Dominque Wilkins, Charles Barkley, Dennis Rodman, Shaquille O'Neal, Kobe Bryant, Nate Robinson, LeBron James and Russell Westbrook. As you can see, I enjoy extremely colorful characters rather than *vanilla* ones like Tim Duncan and John Stockton, no matter how great they are.

Kendrick Perkins: Arrested for Disorderly Conduct and Public Intoxication in August of 2011 as well as for Assault in October, 2013. Perkins currently plays for the NBA's Oklahoma City Thunder.

Kyle Lowry: Was charged with and pleaded *no contest* to battery after verbally abusing and physically throwing a basketball at a female referee during a charity basketball game in Las Vegas. Lowry played for the NBA's Toronto Raptors last season and is expected to be one of the hottest *free agents* on the market this summer.

The above is just a very, very small sampling of charges, arrests and convictions against individuals directly associated with the NBA. For a more complete list, please visit: http://nbacrimelibrary.wordpress.com/

Even the infamous Marge Schott (former owner of MLB's Cincinnati Reds, who famously called two of her best players *million dollar nig**rs,* refused to let her players wear earnings because she believed *only fruits* (i.e. homosexuals, added) *wear earnings*, was accused by former Oakland Athletics executive assistant Sharon Jones of stating, *I would never hire another nig**r. I'd rather have a trained monkey working for me than a nig**r,* before the start of an owners' conference call, and who famously claimed that Adolf Hitler was initially good for Germany, was only suspended for one season (this happened twice). Schott ultimately decided to sell her controlling interest in the Reds, yet even after doing so, she remained a minority owner until her death!

Simply put, I cannot think of a more controversial and seemingly insane reason to slap someone with a lifetime ban, fine them $2.5 million dollars and try to force them to sell their personal possession, than the *he got caught saying politically-incorrect things during a private conversation* line of reasoning. The whole thing is just bizarre.

When I first heard about Sterling's *racist remarks* and the public outcry that followed, my first question was, what exactly did the old coot say, which I would like to think was everyone's initial reaction and first question.

However, it's obvious that the initial reaction for a great many people was simply anger, hatred, vengeance and a desire to see old man Sterling suffer as much as possible. That is a shame.

I remember when Kobe Bryant was interviewed by Ben McGrath of the *New Yorker.* McGrath told Kobe about the Miami Heat players protesting Trayvon Martin's death via Twitter activism and then asked the question, *Is that the kind of thing you could see yourself doing?*

Bryant then gave a very thoughtful reply; a thoughtful reply that he was ripped incessantly for by his peers and the public in general. NFL great Jim Brown attacked him, former CNN contributor Roland Martin insulted him on Twitter, and journalist Jason Whitlock ranted and raved about Bryant on ESPN's *Pardon the Interruption* (PTI), which by the way, is, in my opinion, the best sports-centric television show on the planet. Tony Kornheiser is amazing and can be a voice of clarity with some very profound things to say, when he's not cracking jokes (which generally are also quite funny).

However, what Bryant said was one hundred percent correct, and if my own children grow up to think the same way Kobe Bryant did when he answered Ben McGrath's question, I will be a happy man. For those of you who aren't familiar with Bryant's response, it was as follows:

> *Smartly, I won't react to something just because I'm supposed to, because I'm an African-American. That argument doesn't make any sense to me. So we want to advance as a society and as a culture, but, say, if something happens to an African-American, we immediately come to his defense? Yet you want to talk about how far we've progressed as a society? Well, if we've progressed as a society, then you don't jump to somebody's defense just because they're African-American. You sit and you listen to the facts just like you would in any other situation, right?*

How in the world could anyone, be they Kobe Bryant or Karl Brown from the local grocery store, be ridiculed for such a wise answer? Every single word Kobe said was spot-on, racism-less and wise. If everyone on this planet were to heed Kobe's advice to *listen to the facts* before jumping to conclusions I have no doubt the world would be a safer and more civil place.

The above said, if the world renowned and utterly beloved (at least by Lakers fans, and there are a whole lot of those on this planet) Kobe Bryant can be absolutely lambasted for remarks that were one hundred percent correct, racism-less and wise, just imagine how quickly a vengeance seeking mob could be whipped into a frenzy by Donald Sterling's supposed *Hitler-esque* comments. It didn't take long to find out the answer to such a question, as shortly after Sterling's comments hit the internet, a great many celebrities voiced their opinions, which I will quote below and comment on:

> *There's no room in our society for racism.*
>
> *- Magic Johnson*

What exactly does Magic Johnson mean by this? I agree that racism is idiotic and would go further and state it is both evil and sinful. However, it exists and it isn't going anywhere. Is Magic saying that racists should be *removed* from *society*, and if so, by what means? Should individuals who *think* certain things and utter certain *words* be jailed with people who actually commit crimes like rape and murder? Should they be exiled to Iceland as in Aldous Huxley's *Brave New World* or submitted to torture in a *Ministry of Love* as in George Orwell's *1984*? I for one would like Magic Johnson to explain what he personally feels should be done to individuals who harbor racist thoughts and beliefs. Anyone can expose a problem or condemn an individual but it takes a great deal more thought to actually come up with a realistic solution.

> *Way to go, Commissioner Silver!*
> *The NBA stands for everybody!*
>
> *– Shaquille O'Neal*

I will point out the obvious. Shaquille O'Neal is saying that by banning an 80 year old man who uttered racist words, the NBA proved that it stands for everyone, when what he actually means is that the NBA stands with minorities (as it should). However, the word *everybody* would of course include old white men who think racist thoughts, young men of every race who think sexist thoughts, etc. If men who hold racist beliefs regarding minorities are to be banned from the NBA, does that mean that Black Muslims should never be allowed to attend an NBA game due to their racist beliefs regarding whites (by the way, if Carmelo Anthony is really a member of the extremely racist *Five-Percent Nation*, will he receive a lifetime ban from the league?), various Muslims should never be allowed to attend an NBA game due to their racist beliefs regarding Jews, various Jews should never be allowed to attend an NBA game due to their racist beliefs regarding Muslims, etc.? Either the NBA truly accepts everyone, or they don't, period.

> *Thank you for standing up and leading not only in sport, but setting the example for society to follow!*
>
> *– Isaih Thomas*

My only comment on the above would be that I guess Isaih Thomas feels harboring racist *beliefs* and uttering offensive *words* is much more reprehensible than harboring sexist thoughts and actually *physically* harassing a woman sexually and costing one's employer $11.5 million; interesting.

> *Great move by the @NBA today! #NoPlaceInOurGameForThis #NoPlaceInLifeForThis*
>
> *– J.R. Smith*

My only real comment on the above is that I guess J.R. Smith feels harboring racist *beliefs* and uttering offensive words is much more reprehensible than being *arrested* for reckless driving (which of course could kill someone and not just hurt their feelings), assault, disturbing the peace and destruction of personal property; interesting.

> *I agree 100% with Commissioner Silvers findings and the actions taken against Donald Sterling*
>
> *– Mark Cuban*

I love Mark Cuban and think he's great for the game of basketball. However, he was *charged* by the *SEC* with *insider trading*. I realize he won his court case and I'm glad he did, but the fact remains that Donald Sterling will never be charged with a crime for merely harboring racist thoughts. Again, I would ask if lawful but politically-incorrect *thoughts* and *words* are worse than literal criminal *actions* that various NBA players have committed throughout the years, only to receive a slap on the wrist from the league?

However, let me be clear on what I think of Mark Cuban. I think Cuban is an ingenious businessman and that his *tweet* was a smart business move, period. I do not believe that Mark Cuban actually believes an American citizen should be forced to sell a private possession simply because they said the wrong *words*. However, I do expect Cuban to vote in favor of stripping Sterling of his team, simply because that is the smart business move, even if doing such is extremely hypocritical.

There aren't many individuals on the planet that will do the right thing if they know doing the right thing will cause them to suffer. Jesus Christ of Nazareth was such an individual and many third world individuals who refuse to deny Him even in the face of extreme persecution are such, but for the most part, the vast majority of individuals, let alone billionaire businessmen, will choose the path of least resistance ninety-nine percent of the time.

Regardless of what the media, public and celebrities said about Donald Sterling, the question remains, what exactly did Donald Sterling himself say, and were his words worthy of mere verbal condemnation rather than an actual lifetime ban from the NBA, $2,500,000 fine and apparent stripping of the team he has owned for the past 33 years?

On April 25, 2014, the day before Donald Sterling's 80th birthday (Coincidence? I think not!) *TMZ* – yes the same *TMZ* that has been criticized since its inception for its seemingly unethical and immoral journalism tactics and focus, as well as harangued for purchasing stolen items from the *Indiana Jones and the Kingdom of the Crystal Skull* movie, and even exposed for using a picture from a November 1967 *Playboy* photoshoot and claiming that it was actually a picture of John F. Kennedy on a ship with several nude females – released a recording of a *private* conversation between Los Angeles Clippers owner Donald Sterling and a woman by the name of V. Stiviano (born Maria Vanessa Perez — more on her many aliases later) who is thought to be Sterling's former mistress. This recording can be heard online at: http://www.tmz.com/2014/04/26/donald-sterling-clippers-owner-black-people-racist-audio-magic-johnson/ Two days later the website Deadspin.com released an extra 5:41 recording that picked up where the TMZ recording left off and which can be heard online at: http://deadspin.com/exclusive-the-extended-donald-sterling-tape-1568291249

The TMZ recording lasts for 9:26 and the Deadspin recording lasts for an additional 5:41. However those brief 907 seconds not only cost Donald Sterling his reputation, they may end up costing him well over $320,000,000 when all is said and done, as he is expected to lose that amount in attorney, court and capital gains fees/taxes if the NBA succeeds in forcing him to sell his most prized possession, the Los Angeles Clippers basketball team.

In the aforementioned September 2013 recordings, V. Stiviano says, *I wish I can change the skin, the color of my skin, to which Sterling replies, That isn't the issue. You missed the issue. ... The issue is we don't have to broadcast everything. ... why are you taking pictures with minorities. Why?*

The first thing that stands out to me is that Donald Sterling has no problem with Stiviano being a woman of color (apparently part African-American and part Mexican) and has no issue with the color of her skin. His issue is that she, as his known lover, is broadcasting her relationship with others, and by *others* I believe he meant *men.* Had Sterling simply asked her why she was taking pictures with other *men,* rather than with *minorities*, and stopped there, the insane firestorm of media attention and public outcry that ensued may never have happened. The public could have just chalked up Sterling's words to an old *Sugar-Daddy* being upset with his young mistress for flaunting her relationship with other men, period. Regardless, Sterling did use the word *minorities* and therefore does at least *sound* racist.

However, Stiviano goes on to ask Sterling *what's wrong with black people?* To which he replies, *Nothing, nothing, nothing*.

The above sure doesn't sound like the words of a racist to me, at least not a hood wearing, cross burning *Klan* member like people seem to think Sterling is now. I've met and talked with many people I personally would consider to be *racist*, and I can't recall a single one that would have said there is *nothing* wrong with black people. No, those numbskulls would have ranted and raved about all sorts of idiocy.

Later in the discussion, Stiviano enquires about racism, to which Sterling replies, *there's a culture. People feel certain things. Hispanics feel certain things towards blacks. Blacks feel certain things towards others, groups. It, it's been that way historically, and it will always be that way.* Stiviano later says, *I can't be racist in my heart and Sterling says, And that's good. I'm living in a culture, and I have to live within the culture. So, that's the way it is. That's all I got it. I got the whole message. You live with your heart.*

Sterling never once admitted to being a racist. He merely admits that there is a racist culture around both he and his young mistress. He's right, just as Dominque Wilkins said, racism is still very much alive even in the good ole U.S.A.

Later, Stiviano says, *You want me to have hate towards black people* after Sterling criticizes her for being seen with black people (and again, I believe he specifically means men), apparently because he feels people will look down on her. Sterling replies, *I don't want you to have hate. That's what people do, they turn things around. I want you to love them, privately. In, in your whole life, every day, you can be with them; every single day of your life.*

Again, I've met many racists and it's difficult to imagine even one of them answering the way Sterling answered. How many racists do you know that would answer, *I want you to love them – privately to the question/statement you want me to hate black people?* My guess is none; my guess is that you have never met a single racist that would answer the way Sterling answered.

Later in the discussion Sterling states, *There's no negativity. I love everybody. I'm just saying in your lousy f***ing Instagrams you don't have to have yourself with, walking with black people. You don't have to. If you want to, do it.*

This was one of the gotcha moments in the discussion and one which a lot of people latched unto to prove that Sterling is some sort of reincarnated Adolf Hitler. However, what did the old man actually say? He said he loved *everyone* including *black people* but that he simply didn't approve of his lover having pictures of herself with black people (and again, by people I believe he obviously meant men) on her Instagram account, but that if she wanted to do so, fine, do so. I don't know about you but that does not sound like the ranting of a card carrying *Klan* member; it simply sounds like the words of a scorned *Sugar-Daddy* and typical 80 year old American white male, period.

As soon as Sterling finishes saying *If you want to, do it,* Stiviano hits him with the Larry Bird question and says, *If it's white people, it's okay? If it was Larry Bird, would it have made a difference? to which Sterling replies, You're just a big fighter. I can see; who would want to live with a woman like you? Who would want to live with a woman? All you ever wanted to do is fight. You're a born fighter.*

Okay, one thing is crystal clear, at least in my mind. This entire recorded conversation was an absolute set-up, period. Anyone without a bias can see this. Being a lawyer, Sterling should have recognized the fact that his young mistress was setting him up the minute she brought up *Larry Bird* and *Magic Johnson*. There are no two NBA players in history that provoke a bigger race conversation than Larry Bird and Magic Johnson! Granted, such conversations usually revolve around which player was better, if Larry Bird is only considered as great as he is because of the color of his skin, etc. However, mentioning Magic and Bird in a discussion about racism to an old basketball fan is akin to asking an old baseball fan if he agrees with the statement, *Hank Aaron was a better slugger than Babe Ruth or Derek Jeter was a better ballplayer than Ty Cobb*. Those are questions you simply don't ask an old-timer, not unless you want to have your head bitten off and listen to ranting for the next half an hour. Regardless, I believe that anyone who listens to the full recording should quickly come to the conclusion that this was one big set-up from the beginning.

After bringing up Larry Bird, Stiviano brings up Magic Johnson, explaining that she took a picture with him and admires him. Sterling replies, *I, I think the fact that you admire him, I know him well and he should be admired. And I'm just saying that you're too bad you can't admire him privately and, and during your entire f***ing life your whole life admire him, bring him here, feed him, f**k him, I don't care. You can do anything, but don't put him on the Instagram for the world has to see so they have to call me. And don't bring him into my games? Okay.*

Sterling's above statement seems to be the greatest *gotcha moment* for the press and the public on the first and original TMZ recording, and frankly, that baffles me. The public has latched onto the, *don't bring him to my games* quip while ignoring the context as well as the rest of Sterling's statement. I suppose this shouldn't surprise me as the public often times has a very hard time understanding context, or, like Kobe Bryant said, *listening to the facts.*

The fact is that Donald Sterling specifically said that Magic Johnson *should be admired* but that he personally does not want his known lover posting pictures of herself with Magic or personally bringing him to Clippers games. If this entire conversation is merely a lovers quarrel and the words of an elderly *Sugar-Daddy* who is upset that his young mistress is being called a whore and being accused of sleeping with black men – and specially Magic Johnson – by his circle of friends, than Donald Sterling said little more than what the vast majority of 80 year old Caucasian American *Sugar-Daddy's* would have said (in even far crasser terms) had they believed their young mistress was sleeping around on them and flaunting such indiscretions publicly.

In fact, if this was indeed a lovers quarrel, Donald Sterling said nothing that most men, regardless of their age would have said. Can you imagine a 45 year old restaurant owner who is head over heels with his girlfriend, not exploding on her and using all sorts of crude language, if that girlfriend continuously brought other men – men his buddies thought she was sleeping with – to his restaurant on her lunch breaks, and then posted photos of herself with such men? Of course not!

Sterling concludes the *TMZ* recording with the following words before hanging up, *You're just a fighter and you want to fight.* I agree with the old man's description of Stiviano and I believe it's perfectly clear that V. Stiviano set up Donald Sterling and saw to it that he was publicly crucified by the press and public just as he was about to turn 80 years old. In fact, I'm shocked that anyone who actually listened to the full conversation between Sterling and Stiviano could believe otherwise.

Listen to the long pause Stiviano takes between the words *angry* and *honey* which can be heard from 7: 56-59. Just listen to the last 17 seconds of the conversation as well. Seriously, do yourself a favor and listen to those 17 seconds – from 9:10 – 9:26 – and I believe you will come to the same conclusion I came to, namely, that Donald Sterling is little more than your typical 80 year old Caucasian American man, a man who was upset that his mistress was publicly flaunting her relationship with other men his friends assumed she was sleeping with, a man who was set up by his young mistress simply because he was a billionaire.

Regardless, while I came to the above conclusion after listening to the original *TMZ* recording, when the second extended *Deadspin* recording was released I knew I had to examine that as well. I did exactly that.

One of the first statements V. Stiviano makes on the *extended* recording that really caught my attention, is when she says, *I don't think you're a racist* and continues to say, *I think you have an amazing heart, honey.* I find it amazing that the very woman who apparently set Sterling up for the onslaught of hatred and public vitriol he has received, disagrees with the public and press' opinion that Sterling is a racist at all. She actually believed the exact opposite. In fact, even after the proverbial *s**t hit the fan* and the firestorm started, Stiviano continued to say that she did not feel Sterling was truly a racist; interesting.

The first big *gotcha moment* on the extended recording is when Stiviano asks Sterling, *And are the black Jews less than the white Jews?* and he replies by saying, *A hundred percent, fifty, a hundred percent.* The media and public have claimed that he was personally claiming that black Jews are worth 50-100 percent less than white Jews. However, such is nonsense and nothing more than slander.

The black Jews Sterling is talking about are most likely *Beta Israel*, also known as Ethiopian Jews and perhaps primarily the *Falasha Mura*, who are the descendants of *Beta Israel* who converted to Christianity, which obviously is severely frowned up by Orthodox Jewish believers. Despite various Beta Israel spiritual leaders arguing for the acceptance of the *Falash Mura* by Israel as a whole, the Israeli government decided the *Falasha Mura* can only become citizens if they formally convert to Orthodox Judaism, something many would never even consider, as they would have to deny their Lord and Savior, Jesus Christ of Nazareth, to do so, and such would be unthinkable to a true Christian.

Now, I don't expect *TMZ* and *Deadspin* reporters to have any knowledge of such truths, nor do I expect most NBA beat reporters or even reporters from the major news networks to have any real knowledge of such truths.

However, I do believe there are a great many reporters that understand these truths very well and am saddened that not a single one of them has had the courage to report on this and to make it clear to the raging masses that what Sterling about black Jews may not have been the least bit racist. However, expecting courage in today's day and age is generally an exercise in futility, sadly enough.

Another *gotcha moment* in the extended recording is when Sterling says, *I don't want to change. If my girl can't do what I want, I don't want the girl. I'll find a girl that will do what I want! Believe me. I thought you were that girl—because I tried to do what you want. But you're not that girl,* However, again, I have no idea why such a statement would be connected to racism. This is more a sexist statement than a *racist* one and the sort of belief an enormous amount of athletes and simply men in general hold to. For goodness sake, just listen to the radio for an hour and you can here far, far worse.

Another *gotcha moment* on the extended recording is when Sterling says, *Well then, if you don't feel — don't come to my games. Don't bring black people, and don't come.* However, as I have explained above, I truly believe that when he says *black people* he actually means, *men my friends think you're having sex with,* and if such is indeed what he means, this is not a racist statement either and is little more than the raving of a hurt and angry *Sugar-Daddy* trying to protect his turf and keep his young lover away from those he considers a threat, and nothing more. However, even if Sterling literally and only meant *African American individuals* when he said *black people*, which I do not believe he did, so what? Stiviano was free to ignore him, tell him to shut his mouth and do whatever she wanted to do; that is the beauty of living in America. Of course, if a man can receive a lifetime ban and have his personal possession stripped from him for uttering mere private words, perhaps America is now AmeriKa?

The final and foremost gotcha moment in the extended Deadspin recording comes a short time later in the recording when Stiviano asks Sterling, *Do you know that you have a whole team that's black, that plays for you?* and he answers, *You just, do I know? I support them and give them food, and clothes, and cars, and houses. Who gives it to them? Does someone else give it to them? Do I know that I have — Who makes the game? Do I make the game, or do they make the game? Is there 30 owners, that created the league?*

Boom goes the dynamite! Donald Sterling is the reincarnation of Adolf Hitler! Sterling he needs to have his tongue cut out of his mouth and then be burned at the stake while children watch so they know to never utter such words in the future ... or so the media would have everyone believe. I say ... nonsense!

I agree that Sterling's above comments could one day be found under the definition of the term *plantation mentality*, however that doesn't mean such a definition would be correct (the definition for the word *siphon* has been wrong for over 100 years in the renowned *Oxford English Dictionary*), as what Sterling said is not untrue. Sterling is in fact the owner of the Los Angeles Clippers basketball team and therefore he is indeed the person who pays the player's salaries, which salaries they then use to purchase their homes, cars and the like. If an African American one day purchases an NHL team and has an entire team filled with only Caucasian players and says the exact same thing, I highly doubt anyone would care.

Slave owners did not pay their slaves, let alone pay them wages that allowed them to live like kings, as NBA owners pay their players today. I agree that Sterling's comments can be viewed as racist and are offensive to a great many people. However, I also believe that his words are being viewed as racist, not because the actual statement was in and of itself racist, but merely because it was Donald Sterling who said them.

For example if a Jewish businessman said, *I don't really like dealing with Jews. I'd rather not deal with them at all and wouldn't mind one bit if I never met another one, no one would bat an eyelash.* However if Mahmoud Ahmadinejad said the exact same thing, he would be ridiculed as a nutcase, because we already know he is a nutcase.

All of the above said, below is my personal and full transcript of that infamous September 2013 conversation that *TMZ* leaked, along with the *Deadspin* transcript of the extended interview, minus the irrelevant part where Stiviano is talking to someone in her house named *Lucy.* Please note that I have placed a total of just nine words, namely the phrase *black people* three times, the word *him* twice and the word *minorities* once, in parentheses and quotes. I have also interjected and underlined the exact same phrase, namely, men my friends think you're having sex with, in each of the seven instances. I have done this because I believe it's entirely obvious that the entire conversation between Sterling and Stiviano was nothing more than a quarrel between an old *Sugar-Daddy* and his young lover who just happened to be setting him up for a major fall, after being sued by Sterling's legal wife, and that when Sterling said those words (i.e. *black people, him* and *minorities*) he really did mean, *men my friends think you're having sex with.*

Please put aside any personal bias, pre-conceived notions, anger, pain and the like and just read the below transcript in its entirety. When you're finished reading, be honest with yourself, judge righteously and make up your mind as to whether or not Donald Sterling is truly the *Hitler-esque* racist monster the media has made him out to be, or whether he is little more than a typical 80 year old Caucasian American *Sugar-Daddy*, who uttered private words out of anger in trying to convince his young mistress not to broadcast her relationship with men his friends thought she was having sex with, private words that just happened to become public.

V.S.: Honey, I'm sorry.

D.S.: I'm sorry too.

V.S.: I wish I can change the skin, the color of my skin.

D.S.: That isn't the issue. You missed the issue.

V.S.: What's the issue?

D.S.: The issue is we don't have to broadcast everything.

V.S.: I'm not broadcasting anything. I don't do anything wrong.

D.S.: Nobody said you did anything wrong.

V.S.: I don't do anything wrong. If we ever have any issues, it's because people call you and tell you things about me that are not true.

D.S.: Then why are you broadcasting.

V.S.: I'm not broadcasting anything.

D.S.: Then why are you taking pictures *with men my friends think you're having sex with* (instead of "minorities.") Why?

V.S.: What's wrong with minorities? What's wrong with black people?

D.S.: Nothing, nothing, nothing.

V.S.: What's wrong with Hispanics?

D.S.: It's like talking to an enemy. Unh-uh, there's nothing wrong with minorities. They're fabulous, fabulous, because you're an enemy to me.

V.S.: Why?

D.S.: Because you don't understand.

V.S.: I don't understand what?

D.S.: Nothing, nothing.

V.S.: That racism still is alive?

D.S.: No, but there's a culture.

V.S.: What culture?

D.S.: People feel certain things. Hispanics feel certain things towards blacks. Blacks feel certain things towards others, groups. It, it's been that way historically, and it will always be that way.

V.S.: But it's not that way in my heart and in my mind.

D.S.: But maybe you want to adjust to the world.

V.S.: But why if the world doesn't do anything for me, and they don't make me happy.

D.S.: You're right. I don't want to argue with you. I don't want to argue.

V.S.: I can't be racist in my heart.

D.S.: And that's good. I'm living in a culture, and I have to live within the culture. So, that's the way it is. That's all I got it. I got the whole message. You live with your heart.

V.S.: I don't, you're, you're —

D.S.: You can't be flexible. You can't.

V.S.: I am flexible. I understand that that's the way you were raised, and that's your culture; I'm respectful and —

D.S.: Well, why, why do you have to disrespect them. Those are —

V.S.: Who am I disrespecting?

D.S.: The world before you.

V.S.: Why am I disrespecting them?

D.S.: By, by, by, walking and you're perceived as either a Latina or a white girl. Why can't you be walking publicly with black people, why? Is there a benefit to you?

V.S.: Is it a benefit to me? Does it matter if they're white or blue or yellow?

D.S.: Well, I guess that you don't know that. Maybe you're stupid. Maybe you don't know, what people think of you. It does matter, yeah. It matters.

V.S.: Do you know that I'm mixed?

D.S.: No I don't know it.

V.S.: You know that I'm mixed.

D.S.: You told me you were going to remove those. You said, 'Yes, I understand you.' I mean you change from day to day. Wow; so painful, wow.

V.S.: People call you and tell you that I have black people on my Instagram. And it bothers you.

D.S.: Yeah, it bothers me a lot that you want ah broadcast that you're associating with *men my friends think you're having sex with* (instead of "black people"). Do you have to?

V.S.: You associate with black people.

D.S.: I'm not you and you're not me. You're supposed to be a delicate white or a delicate Latina girl.

V.S.: I'm a mixed girl.

D.S.: Ok well –

V.S.: And you're in love with me; and I'm black and Mexican, whether you like it or not, whether the world accepts it or not. And you're asking me to remove something that's part of me and in my bloodstream. Because the world thinks different of me and you're afraid of what they're going to think, because of your upbringing. You want me to have hate towards black people.

D.S.: I don't want you to have hate. That's what people do, they turn things around. I want you to love them, privately. In, in your whole life, every day, you can be with them; every single day of your life.

V.S.: But not in public?

D.S.: But why publicize it on, on the Instagram and, and why bring it to my games?

V.S.: Why bring the black people to the games? I —

D.S.: I, I don't even wanna discuss anymore. It's over. I don't want to talk about it.

V.S.: I'm sorry that you feel that way.

D.S.: I, I feel that way so strongly, and it may cause our relationship to just break apart. And if it does, it does. It's better to break apart now than to break apart later.

V.S.: I'm sorry that you still have people around you that are full of racism and hate in their heart. I'm sorry that you're still racist in your heart. I'm sorry that you live in a world that's still —

D.S.: How about the, how about your whole life, every day you could do whatever you want. You could sleep with them. You could bring em in, you could do whatever you want. The little I ask you is not to promote it on that, and, and not to bring em to my games.

V.S.: I don't bring anyone to the games.

D.S.: Okay then, there's nothing to argue about.

V.S.: I know.

D.S.: Okay we've got a big problem here. I, I, I really don't feel like going anywhere. I don't feel like going to Europe. I don't feel like just going through the whole thing. We've just, we've got a big problem. If you didn't like someone I was with I would just, stop seeing that person and —

V.S.: I'm sorry I don't have any more friends. What would you like me to do; remove the skin color out of my skin?

D.S.: Is that ah, a real issue or are you making something up?

V.S.: I mean, I just don't understand what the issue is.

D.S.: There's nothing with you or your, your skin color. Why are you saying these things, to upset me? Okay.

V.S.: Sweetie, I'm sorry.

D.S.: I'm so sorry too. We made a giant mistake; both of us. Everything you say to me is so painful. Do I want you to change the color of your skin? You know how to really hurt somebody. And just, instead of saying, 'I, I understand.'

V.S.: I don't understand how you can have so much hate towards minorities.

D.S.: I don't have any hate on nothing.

V.S.: I do not understand —

D.S.: Why would you say I hate —

V.S.: How a person like you who's elevated, who's here, still feels above the world and you can't even be seen with someone in which is considered of a different skin color.

D.S.: They can be with me all day long and all night long.

V.S.: I can't believe that a man who's educated, a man who's a scholar, a man —

D.S.: Well believe it and stop talking about it. Let's finish our discussion with a period, okay? You're not making any good points. You can't believe this man –

V.S.: You're a good person

D.S.: That's all I am. I'm not a good person in your eyes. If I was a good person, you wouldn't say, you wouldn't say I can't believe this, I can't believe that —

V.S.: What am I supposed to say?

D.S.: Which are all lies. I love the black people.

V.S.: Look at all this negativity coming from you.

D.S.: There's no negativity. I love everybody. I'm just saying in your lousy f***ing Instagrams you don't have to have yourself with, walking with <u>*men my friends think you're having sex with*</u> (instead of "black people"). You don't have to. If you want to, do it.

V.S.: If it's white people, it's okay? If it was Larry Bird, would it have made a difference?

D.S.: You're just a big fighter. I can see; who would want to live with a woman like you? Who would want to live with a woman? All you ever wanted to do is fight. You're a born fighter.

V.S.: I'm sorry that you're mad.

D.S.: Ya have the worst mouth.

V.S.: Why are you so angry, honey? What's wrong?

D.S.: What, why would you bring up Larry Bird, what does he got to do with it? You can walk all night long with your sisters, or your family.

V.S.: I, I saw someone I admire. I admire Magic Johnson.

D.S.: Okay, good.

V.S.: I'm sorry.

D.S.: Okay.

V.S.: He's made a lot of changes for his community, for the world, for the people, for the minorities. He's helped a lot of people.

D.S.: Why are your forcing this down my throat. I'm finished talking to you. I have nothing more to say.

V.S.: And I took a picture with someone I admire.

D.S.: Good.

V.S.: And he happens to be black and I'm sorry.

D.S.: I, I think the fact that you admire him, I know him well and he should be admired. And I'm just saying that you're too bad you can't admire him privately and, and during your entire f***ing life your whole life admire him, bring him here, feed him, f**k him, I don't care. You can do anything, but don't put *men my friends think you're having sex with* (instead of "him") on the Instagram for the world has to see so they have to call me. And don't bring *men my friends think you're having sex with* (instead of "him") into my games? Okay.

V.S.: I don't, I never brought, I don't know him personally.

D.S.: Please leave me alone; please, please.

V.S.: I'm sorry; is there anything that I can do to make you feel better?

D.S.: No you can never make me feel better.

V.S.: I'm sorry.

D.S.: You're just a fighter and you want to fight. (Note: The following is where the *Deadspin*.com transcript takes over, added) And I'm not the man who wants to fight.

V.S.: I'm sorry. I'm sorry sweetie. Everything was OK and perfect.

D.S.: I'm telling you, you told me you were going to remove it, so Dennis, the second Dennis looked at me and that comment.

V.S.: I'm sorry, honey, can I get you a little bit more juice? I don't want to fight with you.

D.S.: Of course you do, you love to fight.

V.S.: I don't fight.

D.S.: That's all you do, you fight with everyone.

V.S.: I'm sorry you feel that way, honey. I don't know how this conversation even came about. You were telling me how people called you, and how they mentioned certain things to you, and how it bothers you.

D.S.: Can't you say "The few Instagrams, I won't, I just –

V.S.: Here you go, honey, a little bit of juice, baby. A little bit of juice for you, honey.

D.S.: Thank you.

V.S.: Honey, if it makes you happy, I will remove all of the black people from my Instagram.

D.S.: You said that before, you said, "I understand."

V.S.: I DID remove the people that were independently on my Instagram that are black.

D.S.: Then why did you start saying that you didn't? You just said that you didn't remove them. You didn't remove every –

V.S.: I didn't remove Matt Kemp and Magic Johnson, but I thought –

D.S.: Why?

V.S.: I thought Matt Kemp is mixed, and he was OK, just like me. He's lighter and whiter than me.

D.S.: Ok.

V.S.: I met his mother.

D.S.: You think I'm a racist, and wouldn't –

V.S.: I don't think you're a racist.

D.S.: Yes you do. Yes you do.

V.S.: I think you, you —

D.S.: Evil heart.

V.S.: I don't think so. I think you have an amazing heart, honey. I think the people around you have poison mind, and have a way of thinking.

D.S.: It's the world! You go to Israel, the blacks are just treated like dogs.

V.S.: So do you have to treat them like that too?

D.S.: The white Jews, there's white Jews and black Jews, do you understand?

V.S.: And are the black Jews less than the white Jews?

D.S.: A hundred percent, fifty, a hundred percent.

V.S.: And is that right?

D.S.: It isn't a question—we don't evaluate what's right and wrong, we live in a society. We live in a culture. We have to live within that culture.

V.S.: But shouldn't we take a stand for what's wrong? And be the change and the difference?

D.S.: I don't want to change the culture, because I can't. It's too big and to [unknown]

V.S.: But you can change yourself.

D.S.: I don't want to change. If my girl can't do what I want, I don't want the girl. I'll find a girl that will do what I want! Believe me. I thought you were that girl—because I tried to do what you want. But you're not that girl.

V.S.: There's no need to get upset. No need to get —

D.S.: I just see what I'm living with, what I'm dealing with.

V.S.: I'm sorry. I didn't do anything!

D.S.: You NEVER do anything, and NEVER do anything wrong.

V.S.: But I didn't do anything!

D.S.: You upset me, and made me crazy.

V.S.: You made yourself upset.

D.S.: No, that's not true. You didn't start off by saying, "Honey, I understand, we're living in a culture, we can't –

V.S.: Because I don't understand. I don't see your views. I wasn't raised the way you were raised.

D.S.: Well then, if you don't feel – don't come to my games. Don't bring men my friends think you're having sex with (instead of "black people"), and don't come.

V.S.: Do you know that you have a whole team that's black, that plays for you?

D.S.: You just, do I know? I support them and give them food, and clothes, and cars, and houses. Who gives it to them? Does someone else give it to them? Do I know that I have – Who makes the game? Do I make the game, or do they make the game? Is there 30 owners, that created the league?

V.S.: I'm not going to bring any black people to the stadium.

D.S.: Is it easy to say that?

V.S.: It's very easy for you to say that.

D.S.: For you to say that.

V.S.: I won't say that, to anyone, ever. I would never ask anyone to not bring someone based on race or color –

D.S.: OK.

V.S.: Or culture.

D.S.: It's like saying, "Let's just persecute and kill all of the Jews."

V.S.: Oh, it's the same thing, right?

D.S.: Isn't it wrong? Wasn't it wrong then? With the Holocaust? And you're Jewish, you understand discrimination.

V.S.: You're a mental case, you're really a mental case. The Holocaust, we're comparing with —

D.S.: Racism! Discrimination.

V.S.: There's no racism here. If you don't want to be — walking — into a basketball game with a certain — person, is that racism?

Having listened (hopefully) to the entire 9: 26 recorded conversation and now having read the entire transcript (hopefully) above, I believe it should be crystal clear to you that Donald Sterling was set up. I believe it should also be crystal clear than the NBA and the public rushed to judgment before, as Kobe Bryant would say, listening to the facts, and that old man Sterling was crucified in the press before even getting to mount a proper defense.

Even Sterling's post-NBA-ban comments during his interview with Anderson Cooper, as idiotic as some of them were, were not racist, but merely malicious, ignorant and self-serving. And, believe me, if NBA owners can be stripped of their teams for being ignorant, malicious and self-serving, the league could be owner-less in short order.

I would also like to briefly discuss this V. Stiviano woman. After TMZ made Donald Sterling's private conversation public, and after he was quickly crucified by the press and public, and after he received a lifetime ban from the NBA, that same TMZ revealed that this V. Stiviano woman had been arrested at least four times in the past and had used at least five different aliases, calling her a true chameleon.

According to TMZ, V. Stiviano, operating under the name of Vanessa Maria Perez was arrested by the LAPD in 2002 for petty theft and was convicted and placed on probation. Later, in 2004, she was arrested by Santa Monica PD for another petty theft and felony burglary.

Later, in 2010, she was arrested by the LAPD again, this time for possession of a controlled substance — a felony. Then, in 2012, operating under the name of Monica Gallegos, she was arrested by CHP for driving under the influence (D.U.I.). In addition to Vanessa Maria Perez and Monica Gallegos, court records show she also used the names Maria Valdez, Maria Vanessa Perez and Mariamonica Perez Gallegos!

By the way (although this has nothing to do with anything), why do criminals use variants of the same name as aliases when they are trying to get away with a crime? That seems ridiculous. I mean, this so-called true chameleon is arrested as Vanessa Maria Perez, so she decides to operate under the name Maria Vanessa Perez? I understand criminals aren't generally the sharpest crayons in the box but if I were to commit a crime under the pseudonym Bryant T. Jordan – and get caught – I wouldn't then say, Ha ha, I am going to be really tricky and operate under the name T. Bryant Jordan; no one will ever suspect me then, bwa ha ha. I mean, really? Criminals are that stupid? Come on!

Anyways, in regards to whether or not it was this notorious true chameleon, V. Stiviano who leaked the recording to the press, I will now quote from a Mail Online exclusive article written by Ryan Parry and Martin Dryan which can be read in full at http://www.dailymail.co.uk/

She (V. Stiviano added) and her lawyer maintain she didn't give the tapes to TMZ and she's 'devastated' by what has happened. But her Instagram account paints a very different picture.

Around the time the legal papers were served by Rochelle's (Donald Sterling's legal wife, who filed suit against Stiviano BEFORE the infamous Sterling recording was mysteriously released to the press, added) lawyers, Stiviano posted several Instagram messages apparently teasing her followers about the big news ahead.

In one, she posted a picture of herself looking through binoculars out to sea in a bikini. The caption read: 'It's all coming out!'

Two weeks ago, she posted a picture of a Tupac track playing on her Bentley's sound system called 'All Eyes on Me'. This could have been meaningless, had it not been for her then attaching the hashtags #wallstreetjournal #newsweekly #randomhouse #publishers #nytimes among many others.

Then she posted others reading: 'SKELETONS IN YOUR CLOSET'; 'ONCE THE BEAR IS UNLEASHED, THERE'S NO STOPPING HER...MAKING MODERN DAY HISTORY'

Most tellingly she posted: 'IT DOESN'T MATTER IF YOUR(sic) BROWN OR WHITE, AS LONG AS: YOUR NOT BLACK...'

Did Donald Sterling tell her that he was going to side with his wife and ask for his gifts back? Did this prompt Stiviano to consider going public?

And was it just about the money? Was Sterling in fact used by the ambitious exhibitionist - last night she said one day she'll be the President of the United States - as a launchpad for introducing us to the weird world of mysterious 'V'?

I think it's incredibly obvious that this V character and true chameleon orchestrated a deft set-up of Donald Sterling. That she has seemed to escape the condemnation of both the press and public, while Sterling has been lambasted from morning to night, is a testament to both the sad state of the media today and the short attention span of a public who would much rather judge and convict now and listen to the facts later.

God's word (i.e. the Bible) states in Proverbs 18: 13, He that answereth a matter before he heareth it, it is folly and shame unto him. However, that is exactly what the press and public do on a daily basis and exactly what was done in this Sterling and Stiviano event that captured the word's attention. Yet, no one seems to be ashamed of such folly and shame, as judging a person innocent until proven guilty seems to be all the rage these days.

The above said, I would now like to return to discussing Donald Sterling. As many know, before the infamous recorded conversation with the true chameleon came out, Mr. Sterling was slated to receive the 2014 Humanitarian Award for his lifetime body of work from the National Association for the Advancement of Colored People (NAACP). Mr. Sterling had also previously hired an African American head coach for his Los Angeles Clippers (there are currently just 7 non-white head coaches in the NBA), and an African American General Manager (there are currently just four non-white General Managers in the NBA) for the Clippers as well.

Would a hard core racist really hire an African American head coach, let alone an African American General Manager? I highly doubt it; I seriously, really, highly, doubt it.

Someone I was debating with on the internet said that Sterling hiring a black General Manager and black head coach is no different than a slave owner putting one of his slaves in charge of being his valet. However, I don't agree.

Slave owners regularly forced one slave in particular to serve as their valet and would never have chosen a slave for such a position if they could have also forced a white man to do the same work for free. However, Donald Sterling could have hired any number of white men to be his General Manager and yet he chose to hire African American Elgin Baylor even though there were very, very few African American General Managers in the NBA at that time (or even now). Sterling also recently hired African American Doc Rivers to be the Clippers head coach when he not only could have hired any number of Caucasian coaches to the same position, but could have done so while also paying them a far lower salary. Doc Rivers is a great coach and Sterling paid him a great salary to lead the Clippers. I honestly do not believe a hard core racist would have done any such thing. Others might, but I do not.

However, does Donald Sterling harbor thoughts and feelings that many would consider to be racist even though he himself doesn't feel he is racist and truly believes he has love for everyone? I would guess he does and would be seriously, really, highly shocked if he didn't. However, I would guess the same about any 80 year old Caucasian American, yet the vast majority of such men have never been publicly torn to shreds by the press, nor is anyone trying to force them to sell their most prized possession.

Finally, I would like to make it extremely clear that I am not defending any of Donald Sterling's comments, views, feelings and the like. I am merely pointing out the inconsistencies in the punishment levied against him when compared to those levied (or not levied) against others, as well as defending his right to believe what he wants, and to be afforded the same level of privacy that anyone else would receive.

I am a Biblical Christian and as such I abhor racism and feel that racism of any kind (as well as sexism and even patriotism for that matter, since we're talking about isms) is idiotic. I sincerely believe that every single man and woman ever created was created in the image of God (see Genesis 1: 26-27) and that all nations are indeed of one blood (see Acts 17: 24-31 and especially verse 26). However, I am not naïve enough to believe that everyone agrees with me, nor am I self-centered enough to believe that everyone should be forced to agree with me. As long as someone's thoughts do not turn into hurtful or criminal actions, there is no reason to force anyone to believe anything!

Should Donald Sterling or anyone else on the planet harbor racist thoughts or feelings? No, not unless they want to be stupid on purpose and have a sad life for no reason. However, should anyone on this planet be forced to believe or feel a certain way? Absolutely not!

By the way, the above statement applies to all beliefs and thoughts. I find it extremely hypocritical for someone to say that it's wrong to publicly condemn and force change upon someone who believes that homosexuality (something God's word condemns in no uncertain terms) is acceptable to God and simply an alternative lifestyle or even that people are born homosexual, but that it is okay to publicly condemn and force change upon someone like Donald Sterling for believing that racism is acceptable and justified. Likewise, I find it just as hypocritical for some religious person of whatever faith or denomination to say that it's wrong to publicly condemn and force change upon someone who believes that racism (something God's word also condemns in no uncertain terms) is acceptable and justified, but that it is okay to publicly condemn someone and force change upon someone who believes homosexuality is acceptable to God and simply an alternative lifestyle or even that people are born homosexual.

Simply put, either everyone must be allowed to hold to their personal beliefs – however absurd – and no one should be forced to change such beliefs, or no one should be allowed to hold any personal beliefs that even one other group of people find offensive and everyone who does hold such a belief should be forced to recant under pain of some form of punishment.

The above said, I think we can all agree, or at least I think we should all agree, that the best course of action would be to allow everyone to hold whatever personal beliefs – however absurd – they wish to hold, rather than trying to force everyone to abandon their personal beliefs and merely conform to some politically-correct new-world version of themselves. As, if the press, public or government itself does indeed try to force people to abandon their personal beliefs and conform to a politically-correct new world version of themselves, there could be the proverbial hell to pay, complete with race riots, looting, mass pandemonium, church bombing, mosque bombings, abortion clinic bombings, governmental assassinations and more. North America could one day look like a devilish mixture of Nazi Germany, 1960s Rwanda and 1970s Uganda with a little bit of Roman Catholicism like Inquisition sprinkled in for good measure. If history has taught us anything, it's that conversion through force never works, always leads to evil and should be avoided at all costs.

If the NBA can slap Donald Sterling with a lifetime ban, a $2.5 million fine and try to strip him of his most prized possession for simply uttering politically-incorrect and racist words during a private conversation, what's to stop them from issuing lifetime bans to players who use words that are disparaging to homosexuals (such as when Kobe Bryant called a referee a fu**ing fa*g*t), or sexist (such as when a massive amount players refer to women as bi**hes or worse), or disparaging to Christians (such as when an NBA player is caught blaspheming loud enough for viewers at home to hear) or any other religious follower, etc.? If the NBA starts handing out lifetime bans to its players and executives, simply because they say the wrong words (let alone if those words were said in private such as in Sterling's case), there isn't a single individual who will be above reproach, for as the Word of God states in James 3: 6-8:

> *And the tongue is a fire, a world of iniquity: so is the tongue among our members, that it defileth the whole body, and setteth on fire the course of nature; and it is set on fire of hell. For every kind of beasts, and of birds, and of serpents, and of things in the sea, is tamed, and hath been tamed of mankind: But the tongue can no man tame; it is an unruly evil, full of deadly poison.*

I believe that actions are more important than words, and that actual crimes are more damning in a public context – and therefore more punishable – than mere beliefs. That said, it is a shock to my sensibilities to see an 80 year old man receiving a stricter punishment than a murderer (Charles E. Smith), rapist (DeShawn Stephenson), wife-beater (Jason Kidd), notorious law breaker (Kendrick Perkins and Metta World Peace) and the like.

Below is a transcript transcript of NBA Commissioner Adam Silver's entire April 29, 2014 statement in which he dropped the hammer on Donald Sterling. Commissioner Silver's words are in italics while my comments are in non-italicized, or rather, normal, text:

> *Shortly after the release of an audio recording this past Saturday morning of a conversation that allegedly included Clippers owner*

> *Donald Sterling, the NBA commenced an investigation, which among other things, included an interview of Mr. Sterling.*
>
> *That investigation is now complete. The central findings of the investigation are that the man whose voice is heard on the recording and on a second recording from the same conversation that was released on Sunday is Mr. Sterling and that the hateful opinions voiced by that man are those of Mr. Sterling.*

Firstly, there is no mention that the recording was of a thought-to-be-private conversation. Secondly, while Commissioner Silver says there were *hateful opinions* on the recording, he must realize that *hateful opinions* are expressed every day on the radio, television, and yes, even the basketball courts of America.

> *The views expressed by Mr. Sterling are deeply offensive and harmful; that they came from an NBA owner only heightens the damage and my personal outrage.*

Firstly, I believe the views Mr. Sterling expressed, if taken in context, were merely that he did not want his young lover associating with, or bringing men who his friends believed she was also sleeping with, to his games; and if this was the case, as I believe it was, such views are neither *offensive* nor *harmful,* but merely the understandable ravings of a hurt *Sugar-Daddy.* Secondly, I believe that most NBA owners and even players and executives harbor some offensive and harmful views, and if they were to be set-up and have their private conversations recorded and released to the public, those individuals would *not* have received *lifetime* bans. Thirdly, some players have publicly said extremely offensive and harmful things, such as the aforementioned use of the term *fu**ing f*g*ot* that Kobe Bryant used during an actual NBA game, yet there was certainly no lifetime suspension, nor should there have been as words are just that, words.

> *Sentiments of this kind are contrary to the principles of inclusion and respect that form the foundation of our diverse, multicultural and multiethnic league.*

Firstly, if the comments Sterling made were merely the angry words of a *Sugar-Daddy* who was upset with his young mistress for bringing men whom his friends felt she was also sleeping with, to his games, and posting pictures with such men on her Instagram account, such comments are not *contrary to the principles of inclusion and respect* and are entirely understandable, explainable and forgivable. I would point to some of Dan Gilbert's outrageous and obscene comments, made after LeBron James left the Cavaliers as a free agent in the summer of 2010.

Secondly, when the Commissioner uses the words *respect* and *multicultural*, as a Christian I would like to say that I do not consider the NBA to be all that respectful of Christians. In nearly every televised game you can hear a player or coach blaspheming, let alone using all manner of curse words, which while I personally do not find anywhere near as offensive as taking the Lord's name in vain, many religious people do. Is the NBA going to start handing out massive fines for players like Kevin Garnett who constantly drop F-bombs and then issue lifetime bans to continuous offenders? I highly doubt it and I certainly wouldn't demand such, as again, such are mere words and not actions.

> *I am personally distraught that the views expressed by Mr. Sterling came from within an institution that has historically taken such a leadership role in matters of race relations and caused current and former players, coaches, fans and partners of the NBA to question their very association with the league.*
>
> *To them, and pioneers of the game like Earl Lloyd, Chuck Cooper, Sweetwater Clifton, the great Bill Russell, and particularly Magic Johnson, I apologize. Accordingly, effective immediately, I am banning Mr. Sterling for life from any association with the Clippers*

> *organization or the NBA. Mr. Sterling may not attend any NBA games or practices. He may not be present at any Clippers facility, and he may not participate in any business or player personnel decisions involving the team*

Of the five NBA legends Commissioner Silver mentioned, only Bill Russell did he refer to as *the great,* and frankly, I find that a little curious. Magic Johnson is undoubtedly the greatest point guard in the history of the game whereas Russell is one of three centers who could be called the *greatest* along with Kareem Abdul-Jabbar and Wilt Chamberlain (and I would personally also include Shaquille O'Neal on this list even if many would not). However, Silver only used the term the great when mentioning Russell.

The primary reason I find Commissioner Silver's use of the term *the great* for Bill Russell, and even the fact that he mentioned Russell at all, when talking about banning Sterling for his words, is because Bill Russell himself has a history of uttering some very racist *words*. In Russell's own book, *Second Wind: The Memories of an Opinionated Man*, Russell stated that some of the young autograph seekers he ran into were, *little monsters out hunting scalps.* Um, wow. I think many Native Americans would find such terminology both offensive and harmful, no?

Also, in a 1963 *Sports Illustrated* article titled, *We are Grown Men Playing a Child's Game* by Gilbert Rogin, Russell is quoted as saying, *I dislike most white people because they are people. As opposed to dislike, I like most black people because they are black.* Um, wow again. I think many white people would find such a statement both *offensive* and *harmful* as well, no?

Is the NBA and Commissioner Adam Silver mulling over whether or not to issue a lifetime ban to Bill Russell, or even to simply rename the *Bill Russell NBA Finals Most Valuable Player Award* to the *Michael Jordan NBA Finals Most Valuable Player Award,* since Jordan does have more Finals MVP trophies than anyone in history; although there is that pesky gambling matter, you know, the one some people seem to feel Jordan was banned from the NBA for, when he mysteriously announced his first retirement and went on his ill-fated baseball sabbatical.

Now, don't get me wrong, I consider Bill Russell a great basketball player, the greatest *winner* in NBA history and have no problem with him being included on any and all NBA-themed *Mount Rushmore* lists, *Greatest-of-All-Time* lists and the like. The guy was amazing. I just find it very strange that Commissioner Sterling would mention Bill Russell while laying the smack down on Donald Sterling for his *private* racist remarks when Bill Russell has made very *public* racist remarks in the past. If Bill Russell is *the great* Bill Russell despite making public racist comments, can Donald Sterling really be *the banned Donald Sterling* for making *private* racist comments? I find that hard to understand.

> *He will also be barred from attending NBA Board of Governors meetings or participating in any other league activity.*

Okay, so let me get this straight. An 80 year old codger who privately uttered racist *words* can never attend an NBA Game but a convicted murderer (Charles E. Smith) and a wife-beater and man who ran into the stands during an NBA game to assault a fan (Ron Artest aka Metta World Peace) were allowed to continue to not just attend NBA games, but to actually play in NBA games and be paid for doing so? I must be missing something? Are this old man's *words* going to give fans physical bruises? Are this old coot's *words* going to literally end a fan's life? This is all so incredibly bizarre.

> *I am also fining Mr. Sterling $2.5 million, the maximum amount allowed under the NBA constitution. These funds will be donated to organizations dedicated to anti-discrimination and tolerance efforts that will be jointly selected by the NBA and its Players Association.*

So, Kobe Bryant who *publicly* called an NBA referee a *fu**ing f*g*ot* in front of millions of viewers received a $100,000 fine but Donald Sterling who *privately* told his young mistress that he didn't want her bringing a black man who his friends believed she was having sex with, to his games, receives a $2.5 million fine and a lifetime ban? Again, I must be missing something? I adore Kobe Bryant; he's my favorite player of all-time, and I could personally care the less whether Donald Sterling fades into obscurity or not, yet even I can see the absurdity and uncalled for heavy-handedness the NBA displayed toward old man Sterling.

> *As for Mr. Sterling's ownership interest in the Clippers, I will urge the Board of Governors to exercise its authority to force a sale of the team and will do everything in my power to ensure that that happens. This has been a painful moment for all members of the NBA family. I appreciate the support and understanding of our players during this process, and I am particularly grateful for the leadership shown by Coach Doc Rivers, Union President Chris Paul and Mayor Kevin Johnson of Sacramento, who has been acting as the players' representative in this matter.*

I can't be the only one who sees the absurdity of this, can I? To try and force a man to sell his most prized possession simply because he uttered *words* (*words* that he thought were private and which he did not intend for the public to ever hear) that aren't socially acceptable, cannot be possibly be legal nor just, nor accepted and even condoned by the public, can they? Such a thing can't possibly happen in America; or, can it?

> *We stand together in condemning Mr. Sterling's views. They simply have no place in the NBA.*

Now the above, I can agree with 100 percent, and I actually applaud Commissioner Silver for this final statement! I simply wish his *final* statement could have been his *entire* statement. I absolutely believe racism should be condemned and I respect the NBA a great deal for saying that racist comments *have no place in the NBA*. I simply cannot understand nor justify a lifetime ban, $2.5 million fine and forced sale of the Clippers simply on the basis that such *words* were uttered.

Of course, had Commissioner Silver merely publicly rebuked Donald Sterling with words and fined him a sensible sum, even $2.5 million dollars, and simply not issued the *lifetime ban*, and made it clear he was also in favor of forcing the old codger to sell his most prized possession; I probably would never have even started writing this book. So, in a way, I'm glad Commissioner Silver did what he did, as it gave me something to write about, which I believe is worthy of being read and seriously pondered by the public at large.

I simply cannot agree with, let alone applaud, Commissioner Silver's stated goal of forcing old man Sterling to sell his team. I just can't do it. I agree that it is in *the best interests of the league* to oust Sterling as owner; I simply cannot agree that it is just nor right to do so.

I also have a severe, and I do mean severe problem with a lifetime ban of any kind in any sport, as such leaves no room for repentance and reconciliation, and that is simply preposterous and absurd. All human beings make mistakes and all should be forgiven if they sincerely amend their ways, period.

I will now close with a simple and sincere prayer:

> *Father God, I ask that Your perfect will be done in the lives of all the Los Angeles Clippers' players, coaches and executives, including owner Donald Sterling. I ask that You touch Mr. Sterling's heart with conviction, righteousness and holiness so that he truly realizes that racism is sinful and despicable in your sight, and so that he may repent sincerely and change his heart.*
>
> *I also ask that You touch the hearts and minds of the Clippers' players, coaches and executives, as well as those of the other twenty-nine NBA owners and all the league executives, so that they too may realize that no man is above reproach, no man has a*

perfect tongue, and no man deserves a lifetime ban that leaves no room for sincere repentance and subsequent sincere forgiveness.

Finally I ask that you bless all of us, your Creation, with the wisdom to judge righteously and to live holy lives filled with love rather than hate.

Your will be done Father; I love you Daddy. In the name of Jesus Christ of Nazareth, Amen

EPILOGUE

As I predicted on Twitter after they won *Game Four* in almost miraculous fashion, the Los Angeles Clippers were eliminated from the playoffs in 6 games by the Oklahoma City Thunder. Now, things get real.

For Clippers fans far and wide, it's no longer about their team merely putting a ball in a basket. Rather, it's now about whether the NBA overstepped their bounds, slapped Donald Sterling with excessive and even malicious penalties and whether or not the league will be legally allowed to *force* the Sterling family to sell the Clippers, or whether the league will be *forced* to allow the Sterling's to retain their ownership in the club.

One thing that is extremely interesting to ponder is, if the NBA succeeds in forcing Sterling to sell the Clippers, who exactly will buy them? One of the reasons this is so interesting to ponder, is because three of the possible buyers mentioned so far are: Magic Johnson, Floyd Mayweather and Oprah Winfrey, none of which have a reputation that is above reproach.

Magic Johnson has been accused of setting Donald Sterling up for a fall, of working in consort with V. Stiviano and of doing all of this so that he could purchase the Clippers himself. I have no idea whether such allegations are true or not as it would not surprise me if they were entirely bogus or spot-on. Regardless, the allegations are out there and if Magic Johnson is the one who ends up buying the Clippers and ten years down the line V. Stiviano comes clean and admits that Magic Johnson had his hand in the entire fiasco and had plotted to become the next owner of the Clippers for some time, will the great Magic Johnson receive a *lifetime ban*, or will everyone just pretend such never happened and accuse Stiviano of lying? Honestly, I could actually see the reaction of many folks being little more than to say, *So what, Donald Sterling deserved to have his team stolen for being a racist.* That is a sad and scary thought indeed.

Floyd Mayweather is a great boxing champion, and in my mind at least, the greatest pound for pound boxer in the history of the sport. However, between 2002-2009 alone, Mayweather pled guilty to two charges of *domestic violence*, was convicted for *misdemeanor battery* and plead *no contest* to *misdemeanor assault and battery. Pretty Boy Floyd* has an extremely sordid past, and to force Donald Sterling out, only to welcome Floyd *Money* Mayweather with open arms, would seem to me, to be akin to an NBA team cutting J.R. Smith in order to sign DeShawn Stevenson. Regardless, I could see the public whopping it up if *Money Mayweather* becomes the next owner of the Clippers, whether such makes any sense or not.

Oprah Winfrey is beloved, absolutely beloved by a great many people world-wide. However, she is not without her detractors and own bizarre history (see the M.J. Stephey *Top 10 Oprah Controversies* slide-show at the TIME website for more info). Perhaps Winfrey's greatest public gaffe was when she conducted an interview with the reporter Will Gompertz of the BBC and stated, *There are still generations of people, older people, who were born and bred and marinated in it, in that prejudice and racism, and they just have to die.*

Just imagine for a minute what the public's reaction would be if Donald Sterling was interviewed by the BBC tomorrow and said, *There are still generations of people, older people, who were born and bred and marinated in it, in that selfish Redskin culture* (or any other racist 3-word phrase dealing with various minorities), *and they just have to die.* I have little doubt that if Sterling said such a thing tomorrow, within thirty seconds, there would be people literally calling for him to be jailed or even put out of his misery!

Now, personally, even as a Caucasian male, I am not offended by Oprah's comments. I choose to believe that she was simply saying she believes racism as a belief will sort of die out when the last individual racist dies, and therefore that she is just naive to think such a thing when racist parents generally raise up racist children. Or, that perhaps she really is a bit racist herself, and if that is the case, that I can simply pray for her and refuse to accept such racist idiocy.

Regardless, Oprah Winfrey did utter those words and even a quick web search will reveal that there are indeed a great many people who found such words extremely *offensive* and *harmful*, the exact terminology used by NBA Commissioner Adam Silver when he reprimanded, condemned, fined and banned Donald Sterling over his own offensive and harmful *words.* However, if Oprah becomes the next owner of the Clippers, I imagine the public will rejoice, regardless of what she said during that *BBC* interview, even if such would be extremely hypocritical.

While there certainly are a great many celebrities and wealthy business men and women that would love to purchase the Los Angeles Clippers, they may be in for a very, very long wait. Donald Sterling has retained the services of renowned antitrust attorney Maxwell M. Blecher and is expected to launch an all-out legal assault against the NBA in the near future. I for one think Sterling has a solid chance of beating the mighty NBA in court as well, though it also would not surprise me at all if political-correctness defeats actually justice, wins the day, and Sterling loses badly.

However, attorney Maxwell M. Blecher has beaten the NBA in court before, when they tried to bully Sterling into moving the Clippers. He has also beaten the extremely powerful NFL before, twice. One victory can be chalked up as an aberration and even two victories can be chalked up to *luck,* but three victories? Three victories is a trend, and at the very least, signifies that Blecher is a force to be reckoned with.

According to his firm's website, attorney Blecher is renowned for his expertise in the antitrust field. He has litigated significant cases resulting in many precedent setting decisions in state and federal courts, including the California and U.S. Supreme Courts. He has testified before Congressional hearings; authored numerous articles on antitrust and civil litigation; and lectures extensively on antitrust and trial practice at programs sponsored by federal, state and local bar associations.

Blecher is also a Fellow of the *American College of Trial Lawyers* and of the *American Board of Trial Advocates*. He served on President Carter's *National Commission for the Review of Antitrust Laws*. In 1998 the California State Bar named him *Antitrust Lawyer of the Year.* Since 1995 he has been listed in *Best Lawyers in America*; profiled in *Chambers USA Guide: America's Leading Business Lawyers*; and is one of 14 attorneys profiled in *America's Top Trial Lawyers*.

Donald Sterling is hoping to defeat the NBA in court and all of the above said, he may be represented by the one man who can turn such a hope into a reality. Simply put, ole Maxwell Blecher ain't no joke!

Of course, human justice is often anything but blind, and many times allows itself to be corrupted by the desire of the masses – even if such desire is neither legal nor just – while divine justice is blind indeed and always just and righteous, even if it does take a long time to come into play in many situations. I can only hope and pray that God's perfect will shall be done on earth as it is in heaven, whatever that may be, and whether I or anyone else understands it or not.

Of course, whether Donald Sterling wins or loses a case against the NBA, he has already served as a mirror for society to gaze into and see their own shortcomings of self-righteousness, hypocrisy, hatred and unforgiveness. I have little doubt that many of the people that have attacked Sterling with the most vitriol are in fact closet racists themselves, and that many others are filled with hatred of one form or another.

However, the thing that may be the most disturbing about this entire fiasco, is the mob mentality of the public, mixed with the idea that someone's inner thoughts and personal beliefs can be forcibly changed or punished, and that those individuals who refuse to change such inner thoughts and personal beliefs, have no place in society. That is a horrifying thought!

From the 11th – 16th centuries the Roman Catholic religion (which is nowhere near synonymous with *Biblical Christianity* or the teachings of Jesus Christ as recorded in the *New Testament*) tried to force Biblical Christians, and quite frankly all non-Catholics, to believe as they believed, under pain of torture and death. Their nearly world-wide reign of terror was responsible for the death of tens of millions!

Many of the victims of the Roman Catholic *Inquisition* and maniacal mass purging of non-Catholics, were in fact tortured and murdered for nothing more than *thinking* the wrong way or uttering the wrong words and not for any actual *actions* they carried out, let alone *crimes* they committed. Would those folks who condemned Donald Sterling like to see elderly men with racist *thoughts* and who from time to time utter racist *words,* treated the same way and expunged from the earth? Sadly, I believe the answer is yes, many of them would like that very much.

Today, nearly the whole word agrees the Roman Catholic *Inquisitions* were unthinkable evils perpetuated upon the human race, yet there are a great many modern day inquisitions that continue to take place on a daily basis. Network presidents have replaced Popes, reporters and bloggers have replaced Inquisitors, and, newspapers, magazines, radio programs, television shows, websites, blogs, podcasts and tweets have replaced the rack, stocks, heretics fork, branks, wheel, iron maiden, head crusher and Judas cradle, while reputations rather than bodies (for the most part) are tortured and murdered in the 21st century. However the pain that such modern inquisitions cause remains palpable.

Renowned novelist and essayist Salman Rushdie had a fatwa requiring his execution (i.e. assassination) issued by the *Supreme Leader of Iran* Ayatollah Ruhollah Khomeini on February 14, 1989. Why? Simply because he authored a book (*The Satanic Verses*) that detailed the time when Islam's prophet Muhammad allowed intercessory prayers to be made to three Pagan Meccan goddesses: All☒t, Uzza, and Man☒t (for more information on this, see: www.answering-islam.org/Responses/Saifullah/sverses.htm).

The mere publication of Rushdie's book (i.e. written *words*) sparked written and verbal attacks (i.e. *words*), which were to be expected and are entirely understandable. However, things quickly got out of hand and before long several individuals who merely had a hand in translating or publishing the book were attacked, seriously injured and even killed, while many others perished in riots in various countries! On September 24, 1998, as a prerequisite to the reinstatement of diplomatic relations with Britain, the Iranian government publicly committed to *neither support nor hinder assassination operations on Rushdie;* however Islamic Iranian hardliners have continued to reaffirm the Ayatollah's original death sentence!

Is this the sort of thing we want to happen in North America? For individuals to be attacked, injured and murdered for merely expressing their thoughts or uttering or writing down mere *words*? I sincerely hope not!

However, I wonder, if Donald Sterling can truly receive a lifetime ban, $2,500,000 fine and be forced, against his will, to sell his most prized personal possession simply because of his own personal *beliefs* (however abhorrent) and the *words* (however offensive) he uttered during a private conversation, what's next?

Will the NBA start banning its players when they utter sexist words and therefore lose half the players in the league to suspension in short order?

Will the American public start physically attacking individuals who *utter* politically-incorrect *beliefs*?

Will individuals who *believe* and have *written* or *stated* that homosexuality is sinful, be suspended from their jobs or be physically attacked, even if they have never discriminated against homosexuals?

Will parents who *believe* in *creationism* or practice *homeschooling* lose their parental rights?

Will the U.S. citizens who *write* or *speak* against one of the government's controversial policies be forced by the government to sell their businesses or homes and live in a prescribed area?

Will overzealous pro-lifers start bombing the offices of doctors who have never actually performed an abortion, merely because they have *written* pro-choice material?

Will overzealous pro-choicers start killing pro-lifers who would never dream of doing nything other than protesting with *words* on picket signs?

Will *Down's syndrome* be eradicated from North America, not because a cure was found, but because every single Down syndrome in the womb was aborted, even against the mother's wishes?

Will large members of one religion start killing large members of another religion on North American soil, simply for having different *beliefs*?

Will James Demanaco's film *The Purge* become a reality?

Many people will read the above list and think, *those things will never happen*, however some of those things are already happening in America and Canada, while a great many of them occur on a daily basis in many countries around the world. And, lest we forget, Germany was not some third world country with an uneducated public and under Sharia or any other religion-based law.

Germany had a highly educated citizenry, was a cultural center, a true first world country, and yet a massive amount of its citizens were slaughtered in cold blood while that educated and advanced citizenry went about their daily lives as if nothing was happening. Anyone who thinks another *Holocaust* could never happen in North America is naive, period. As long as darkness remains in the heart of man, the possibility of almost unimaginable horror exists.

Those who mercilessly condemned Donald Sterling did so while also exposing the darkness in their own hearts, a darkness they are at risk of never being forgiven of. As Martin Luther King, Jr. said, *there is some good in the worst of us and evil in the best of us. When we discover this, we are less prone to hate our enemies, and as the poet Tupac Shakur said, it takes skill to be real, time to heal each other,* and as Your Creator and Savior Jesus Christ of Nazareth said, *if ye forgive not men their trespasses, neither will your Father forgive your trespasses*. Now is the time for all of us to realize there is both good and evil in every adult on this planet, stop hating our enemies, truly *forgive* them and ultimately be *real* and skilfully *heal* others.

Is Donald Sterling an *innocent* human being? Of course not! However, neither are you or anyone else reading this book; and that dear reader is the point. We all sin, and therefore, we should all truly repent and truly forgive.

COMPLETE TRANSCRIPT OF THE STERLING RECORDINGS

Below is my personal and full transcript of the infamous September 2013 conversation, released by TMZ, between Donald Sterling and the true chameleon now operating under the name V. Stiviano, along with the Deadspin transcript of the extended conversation, minus the irrelevant part where Stiviano is talking to someone in her house named Lucy.

V.S.: Honey, I'm sorry.

D.S.: I'm sorry too.

V.S.: I wish I can change the skin, the color of my skin.

D.S.: That isn't the issue. You missed the issue.

V.S.: What's the issue?

D.S.: The issue is we don't have to broadcast everything.

V.S.: I'm not broadcasting anything. I don't do anything wrong.

D.S.: Nobody said you did anything wrong.

V.S.: I don't do anything wrong. If we ever have any issues, it's because people call you and tell you things about me that are not true.

D.S.: Then why are you broadcasting.

V.S.: I'm not broadcasting anything.

D.S.: Then why are you taking pictures with minorities. Why?

V.S.: What's wrong with minorities? What's wrong with black people?

D.S.: Nothing, nothing, nothing.

V.S.: What's wrong with Hispanics?

D.S.: It's like talking to an enemy. Unh-uh, there's nothing wrong with minorities. They're fabulous, fabulous, because you're an enemy to me.

V.S.: Why?

D.S.: Because you don't understand.

V.S.: I don't understand what?

D.S.: Nothing, nothing.

V.S.: That racism still is alive?

D.S.: No, but there's a culture.

V.S.: What culture?

D.S.: People feel certain things. Hispanics feel certain things towards blacks. Blacks feel certain things towards others, groups. It, it's been that way historically, and it will always be that way.

V.S.: But it's not that way in my heart and in my mind.

D.S.: But maybe you want to adjust to the world.

V.S.: But why if the world doesn't do anything for me, and they don't make me happy.

D.S.: You're right. I don't want to argue with you. I don't want to argue.

V.S.: I can't be racist in my heart.

D.S.: And that's good. I'm living in a culture, and I have to live within the culture. So, that's the way it is. That's all I got it. I got the whole message. You live with your heart.

V.S.: I don't, you're, you're —

D.S.: You can't be flexible. You can't.

V.S.: I am flexible. I understand that that's the way you were raised, and that's your culture; I'm respectful and —

D.S.: Well, why, why do you have to disrespect them. Those are —

V.S.: Who am I disrespecting?

D.S.: The world before you.

V.S.: Why am I disrespecting them?

D.S.: By, by, by, walking and you're perceived as either a Latina or a white girl. Why can't you be walking publicly with black people, why? Is there a benefit to you?

V.S.: Is it a benefit to me? Does it matter if they're white or blue or yellow?

D.S.: Well, I guess that you don't know that. Maybe you're stupid. Maybe you don't know, what people think of you. It does matter, yeah. It matters.

V.S.: Do you know that I'm mixed?

D.S.: No I don't know it.

V.S.: You know that I'm mixed.

D.S.: You told me you were going to remove those. You said, 'Yes, I understand you.' I mean you change from day to day. Wow; so painful, wow.

V.S.: People call you and tell you that I have black people on my Instagram. And it bothers you.

D.S.: Yeah, it bothers me a lot that you want ah broadcast that you're associating with black people. Do you have to?

V.S.: You associate with black people.

D.S.: I'm not you and you're not me. You're supposed to be a delicate white or a delicate Latina girl.

V.S.: I'm a mixed girl.

D.S.: Ok well –

V.S.: And you're in love with me; and I'm black and Mexican, whether you like it or not, whether the world accepts it or not. And you're asking me to remove something that's part of me and in my bloodstream. Because the world thinks different of me and you're afraid of what they're going to think, because of your upbringing. You want me to have hate towards black people.

D.S.: I don't want you to have hate. That's what people do, they turn things around. I want you to love them, privately. In, in your whole life, every day, you can be with them; every single day of your life.

V.S.: But not in public?

D.S.: But why publicize it on, on the Instagram and, and why bring it to my games?

V.S.: Why bring the black people to the games? I —

D.S.: I, I don't even wanna discuss anymore. It's over. I don't want to talk about it.

V.S.: I'm sorry that you feel that way.

D.S.: I, I feel that way so strongly, and it may cause our relationship to just break apart. And if it does, it does. It's better to break apart now than to break apart later.

V.S.: I'm sorry that you still have people around you that are full of racism and hate in their heart. I'm sorry that you're still racist in your heart. I'm sorry that you live in a world that's still —

D.S.: How about the, how about your whole life, every day you could do whatever you want. You could sleep with them. You could bring em in, you could do whatever you want. The little I ask you is not to promote it on that, and, and not to bring em to my games.

V.S.: I don't bring anyone to the games.

D.S.: Okay then, there's nothing to argue about.

V.S.: I know.

D.S.: Okay we've got a big problem here. I, I, I really don't feel like going anywhere. I don't feel like going to Europe. I don't feel like just going through the whole thing. We've just, we've got a big problem. If you didn't like someone I was with I would just, stop seeing that person and —

V.S.: I'm sorry I don't have any more friends. What would you like me to do; remove the skin color out of my skin?

D.S.: Is that ah, a real issue or are you making something up?

V.S.: I mean, I just don't understand what the issue is.

D.S.: There's nothing with you or your, your skin color. Why are you saying these things, to upset me? Okay.

V.S.: Sweetie, I'm sorry.

D.S.: I'm so sorry too. We made a giant mistake; both of us. Everything you say to me is so painful. Do I want you to change the color of your skin? You know how to really hurt somebody. And just, instead of saying, 'I, I understand.'

V.S.: I don't understand how you can have so much hate towards minorities.

D.S.: I don't have any hate on nothing.

V.S.: I do not understand –

D.S.: Why would you say I hate –

V.S.: How a person like you who's elevated, who's here, still feels above the world and you can't even be seen with someone in which is considered of a different skin color.

D.S.: They can be with me all day long and all night long.

V.S.: I can't believe that a man who's educated, a man who's a scholar, a man –

D.S.: Well believe it and stop talking about it. Let's finish our discussion with a period, okay? You're not making any good points. You can't believe this man –

V.S.: You're a good person

D.S.: That's all I am. I'm not a good person in your eyes. If I was a good person, you wouldn't say, you wouldn't say I can't believe this, I can't believe that –

V.S.: What am I supposed to say?

D.S.: Which are all lies. I love the black people.

V.S.: Look at all this negativity coming from you.

D.S.: There's no negativity. I love everybody. I'm just saying in your lousy f***ing Instagrams you don't have to have yourself with, walking with black people. You don't have to. If you want to, do it.

V.S.: If it's white people, it's okay? If it was Larry Bird, would it have made a difference?

D.S.: You're just a big fighter. I can see; who would want to live with a woman like you? Who would want to live with a woman? All you ever wanted to do is fight. You're a born fighter.

V.S.: I'm sorry that you're mad.

D.S.: Ya have the worst mouth.

V.S.: Why are you so angry, honey? What's wrong?

D.S.: What, why would you bring up Larry Bird, what does he got to do with it? You can walk all night long with your sisters, or your family.

V.S.: I, I saw someone I admire. I admire Magic Johnson.

D.S.: Okay, good.

V.S.: I'm sorry.

D.S.: Okay.

V.S.: He's made a lot of changes for his community, for the world, for the people, for the minorities. He's helped a lot of people.

D.S.: Why are your forcing this down my throat. I'm finished talking to you. I have nothing more to say.

V.S.: And I took a picture with someone I admire.

D.S.: Good.

V.S.: And he happens to be black and I'm sorry.

D.S.: I, I think the fact that you admire him, I know him well and he should be admired. And I'm just saying that you're too bad you can't admire him privately and, and during your entire f***ing life your whole life admire him, bring him here, feed him, f**k him, I don't care. You can do anything, but don't put him on the Instagram for the world has to see so they have to call me. And don't bring him into my games? Okay.

V.S.: I don't, I never brought, I don't know him personally.

D.S.: Please leave me alone; please, please.

V.S.: I'm sorry; is there anything that I can do to make you feel better?

D.S.: No you can never make me feel better.

V.S.: I'm sorry.

D.S.: You're just a fighter and you want to fight. And I'm not the man who wants to fight.

V.S.: I'm sorry. I'm sorry sweetie. Everything was OK and perfect.

D.S.: I'm telling you, you told me you were going to remove it, so Dennis, the second Dennis looked at me and that comment.

V.S.: I'm sorry, honey, can I get you a little bit more juice? I don't want to fight with you.

D.S.: Of course you do, you love to fight.

V.S.: I don't fight.

D.S.: That's all you do, you fight with everyone.

V.S.: I'm sorry you feel that way, honey. I don't know how this conversation even came about. You were telling me how people called you, and how they mentioned certain things to you, and how it bothers you.

D.S.: Can't you say "The few Instagrams, I won't, I just –

V.S.: Here you go, honey, a little bit of juice, baby. A little bit of juice for you, honey.

D.S.: Thank you.

V.S.: Honey, if it makes you happy, I will remove all of the black people from my Instagram.

D.S.: You said that before, you said, "I understand."

V.S.: I DID remove the people that were independently on my Instagram that are black.

D.S.: Then why did you start saying that you didn't? You just said that you didn't remove them. You didn't remove every –

V.S.: I didn't remove Matt Kemp and Magic Johnson, but I thought –

D.S.: Why?

V.S.: I thought Matt Kemp is mixed, and he was OK, just like me. He's lighter and whiter than me.

D.S.: Ok.

V.S.: I met his mother.

D.S.: You think I'm a racist, and wouldn't –

V.S.: I don't think you're a racist.

D.S.: Yes you do. Yes you do.

V.S.: I think you, you –

D.S.: Evil heart.

V.S.: I don't think so. I think you have an amazing heart, honey. I think the people around you have poison mind, and have a way of thinking.

D.S.: It's the world! You go to Israel, the blacks are just treated like dogs.

V.S.: So do you have to treat them like that too?

D.S.: The white Jews, there's white Jews and black Jews, do you understand?

V.S.: And are the black Jews less than the white Jews?

D.S.: A hundred percent, fifty, a hundred percent.

V.S.: And is that right?

D.S.: It isn't a question—we don't evaluate what's right and wrong, we live in a society. We live in a culture. We have to live within that culture.

V.S.: But shouldn't we take a stand for what's wrong? And be the change and the difference?

D.S.: I don't want to change the culture, because I can't. It's too big and to [unknown]

V.S.: But you can change yourself.

D.S.: I don't want to change. If my girl can't do what I want, I don't want the girl. I'll find a girl that will do what I want! Believe me. I thought you were that girl—because I tried to do what you want. But you're not that girl.

V.S.: There's no need to get upset. No need to get —

D.S.: I just see what I'm living with, what I'm dealing with.

V.S.: I'm sorry. I didn't do anything!

D.S.: You NEVER do anything, and NEVER do anything wrong.

V.S.: But I didn't do anything!

D.S.: You upset me, and made me crazy.

V.S.: You made yourself upset.

D.S.: No, that's not true. You didn't start off by saying, "Honey, I understand, we're living in a culture, we can't —

V.S.: Because I don't understand. I don't see your views. I wasn't raised the way you were raised.

D.S.: Well then, if you don't feel — don't come to my games. Don't bring black people, and don't come.

V.S.: Do you know that you have a whole team that's black, that plays for you?

D.S.: You just, do I know? I support them and give them food, and clothes, and cars, and houses. Who gives it to them? Does someone else give it to them? Do I know that I have — Who makes the game? Do I make the game, or do they make the game? Is there 30 owners, that created the league?

V.S.: I'm not going to bring any black people to the stadium.

D.S.: Is it easy to say that?

V.S.: It's very easy for you to say that.

D.S.: For you to say that.

V.S.: I won't say that, to anyone, ever. I would never ask anyone to not bring someone based on race or color —

D.S.: OK.

V.S.: Or culture.

D.S.: It's like saying, "Let's just persecute and kill all of the Jews."

V.S.: Oh, it's the same thing, right?

D.S.: Isn't it wrong? Wasn't it wrong then? With the Holocaust? And you're Jewish, you understand discrimination.

V.S.: You're a mental case, you're really a mental case. The Holocaust, we're comparing with –

D.S.: Racism! Discrimination.

V.S.: There's no racism here. If you don't want to be – walking – into a basketball game with a certain – person, is that racism?

COMPLETE TRANSCRIPT OF ADAM SILVER'S NEWS CONFERENCE

I would like to thank USA Today Sports for making the following transcript available on-line and in a very timely manner:

> **ADAM SILVER:** Shortly after the release of an audio recording this past Saturday morning of a conversation that allegedly included Clippers owner Donald Sterling, the NBA commenced an investigation, which among other things, included an interview of Mr. Sterling.
>
> That investigation is now complete. The central findings of the investigation are that the man whose voice is heard on the recording and on a second recording from the same conversation that was released on Sunday is Mr. Sterling and that the hateful opinions voiced by that man are those of Mr. Sterling.

The views expressed by Mr. Sterling are deeply offensive and harmful; that they came from an NBA owner only heightens the damage and my personal outrage.

Sentiments of this kind are contrary to the principles of inclusion and respect that form the foundation of our diverse, multicultural and multiethnic league.

I am personally distraught that the views expressed by Mr. Sterling came from within an institution that has historically taken such a leadership role in matters of race relations and caused current and former players, coaches, fans and partners of the NBA to question their very association with the league.

To them, and pioneers of the game like Earl Lloyd, Chuck Cooper, Sweetwater Clifton, the great Bill Russell, and particularly Magic Johnson, I apologize. Accordingly, effective immediately, I am banning Mr. Sterling for life from any association with the Clippers organization or the NBA. Mr. Sterling may not attend any NBA games or practices. He may not be present at any Clippers facility, and he may not participate in any business or player personnel decisions involving the team.

He will also be barred from attending NBA Board of Governors meetings or participating in any other league activity.

I am also fining Mr. Sterling $2.5 million, the maximum amount allowed under the NBA constitution. These funds will be donated to organizations dedicated to anti-discrimination and tolerance efforts that will be jointly selected by the NBA and its Players Association.

As for Mr. Sterling's ownership interest in the Clippers, I will urge the Board of Governors to exercise its authority to force a sale of the team and will do everything in my power to ensure that that happens. This has been a painful moment for all members of the NBA family. I appreciate the support and understanding of our players during this process, and I am particularly grateful for the leadership shown by Coach Doc Rivers, Union President Chris Paul and Mayor Kevin Johnson of Sacramento, who has been acting as the players' representative in this matter.

We stand together in condemning Mr. Sterling's views. They simply have no place in the NBA.

Thank you, and I'll take any questions.

Q. Do you or any of your emissaries have any clue as to whether Mr. Sterling will acquiesce to your wishes to sell the team, or do you expect a fight?

ADAM SILVER: I have no idea.

Q. From polling the owners that you've spoken to, what support do you think you have to force Mr. Sterling to sell the team?

ADAM SILVER: I didn't poll the owners. I spoke to several owners, and I have their full support.

Q. What kind of authority do they have to force a sale?

ADAM SILVER: The owners have the authority subject to three quarters vote of the ownership group, of the partners, to remove him as an owner.

Q. The word you used specifically was outrage. You said that you were personally outraged, yet many people believe that they are outraged that for years people have known that this man is a racist slumlord and the NBA hasn't done anything until today. Can you please answer why.

ADAM SILVER: I can't speak to past actions other than to say that when specific evidence was brought to the NBA, we acted.

Q. Should someone lose their team for remarks shared in private as this is a slippery slope?

ADAM SILVER: Whether or not these remarks were initially shared in private, they are now public, and they represent his views.

Q. What was the process to coming to this decision over the last couple days, and when did you decide that this was the appropriate action to take?

ADAM SILVER: I ultimately decided this morning that this was the appropriate action, and the process beginning Saturday morning when this tape was first released was to appoint an investigator. It was David Anders from the Wachtell Lipton firm. He conducted a series of interviews, some by phone, some in person. He concluded his investigation late last night.

Q. Adam, you said you would encourage owners to force the sale of the Clippers. When will that action take place?

ADAM SILVER: The process will begin immediately. We will most likely use a standing committee of the NBA. The equivalent of our executive committee is our advisory finance committee. I've had several discussions with Glen Taylor, who is our chairman of the board and also the leader of the advisory finance committee, and we will begin that process immediately.

Q. In your conversations with Sterling, did he own up to this immediately? Was it only after you guys had come up with some sort of proof? And what, if anything, has he expressed approaching remorse, regret, anything? What's his sentiment at this point?

ADAM SILVER: Mr. Sterling acknowledged it was his voice on the tape, and he has not expressed to me directly any other views.

Q. What message do you have for the Clippers and their fans and their fan base in terms of moving forward from this point on?

ADAM SILVER: My message to the Clippers fans is this league is far bigger than any one owner, any one coach, any one player. This institution has been around for a long time, and it will stand for a long time, and I have complete confidence in Doc Rivers, in the basketball management of that club, and the players deserve their support. They've just been through an incredibly difficult incident in their lives.

Q. Was the punishment designed in effect to get the message across to Mr. Sterling that there's no point in him there's no advantage, nothing to be gained from him continuing his ownership? And also in determining what the punishment would be, including the suggestion to the Board of Governors, did you take into account Mr. Sterling's past behavior, or was it just based on this one particular incident?

ADAM SILVER: In meting out this punishment we did not take into account his past behavior. When the board ultimately considers his overall fitness to be an owner in the NBA, they will take into account a lifetime of behavior.

Q. Adam, could you just explain or lay out for us what specific power in the constitution and bylaws you exercised with your ban, and what specific was it a broad violation or a specific violation, and with respect to the forced sale, what specific section of the constitution covers that, and is that a broad violation or a specific one?

ADAM SILVER: I'll let the lawyers lay out for you the specific provisions of our constitution. Let's just leave it that we have the authority to act as I've recommended.

Q. Is the NBA considering more African American ownership at this point?

ADAM SILVER: We're always open to ownership from people of all races, nationalities, ethnicities. As you know we have an African American primary owner in the league right now. Shaquille O'Neal just became a small owner of the Sacramento Kings. David Robinson is an owner of the San Antonio Spurs. Vivek Ranadive, a person of color born in Mumbai, India, just became the primary owner of the Sacramento Kings. So I believe we have a very diverse league, but I'd always like to see it become more diverse.

Q. What about Magic Johnson? Is that an option at this point?

ADAM SILVER: Magic Johnson knows he's always welcome as an owner in this league. He's been a part owner in the past of the Los Angeles Lakers, and he's always welcome and a close friend of the NBA family.

Q. Did you talk to any of the players before you came to this decision? And what about Clippers' players; if they do not want to play for a team owned by Donald Sterling anymore, do they have any recourse?

ADAM SILVER: I talked to several players before rendering my decision. Coincidentally I'd had a trip planned for this weekend. I was in Memphis for a game. I was in Oakland, and then I was in Portland Sunday night for games. I had a chance to talk directly to Chris Paul. I spoke to other members of the team. I spoke extensively to Doc Rivers, and as I said, Kevin Johnson has been representing the players' interests, and he and I have been talking multiple times a day.

So I believe the players will be satisfied with the decision and the renderings that we've made today. If a player in the future doesn't want to play for the Los Angeles Clippers and he's under contract, we'll deal with that when it happens. But that's not my sense of where we are right now.

Q. Will this situation cause you moving forward to put new rules in place for owners from the NBA?

ADAM SILVER: I'm not sure. I mean, we're always willing to take a fresh look at our rules, our constitution and bylaws, but I believe we have appropriate rules in place right now to cover a situation like this.

Q. Just to be clear, you said when specific evidence was brought to the league you did act. In past cases, has Donald Sterling ever been fined or suspended for racial or offensive remarks, and if not, why not?

ADAM SILVER: He's never been suspended or fined by the league because while there have been well documented rumors and cases filed, he was sued and the plaintiff lost the lawsuit. That was Elgin Baylor. There was a case brought by the Department of Justice in which ultimately Donald Sterling settled and there was no finding of guilt, and those are the only cases that have been brought to our attention. When those two litigations were brought, they were followed closely by the league office.

Q. Just a follow to that, one of the greatest players of all time, Elgin Baylor, accused Donald Sterling of running a plantation style franchise. Did that not concern you, and why was that not investigated? Despite the fact he lost the case, he has a prominent standing in the league and he said some very serious things.

ADAM SILVER: It concerned us greatly. We followed the litigation closely, and ultimately Elgin Baylor did not prevail in that litigation.

Q. Obviously Carmax and State Farm withdrew their sponsorship with the LA Clippers. With you as the commissioner of the NBA, what would you tell other people who are maybe on the fence or who have withdrawn who in the future might want to invest in one of your franchises?

ADAM SILVER: I would say those marketing partners of the Clippers and partners of the entire NBA should judge us by our response to this incident, and I think we've responded appropriately, and I would be hopeful that they would return into their business relationships with the Clippers.

Q. I'm wondering if you've spoken to Mr. Sterling about this ban or any of his representatives, and if so, what has Mr. Sterling's reaction been to the punishment?

ADAM SILVER: I did not speak directly to his representatives about this ban. They were informed shortly before this press conference. I did not hear precisely what their reaction was.

Q. Have there been any decisions about whether the immediate members of Mr. Sterling's family, including Rochelle, will be allowed to remain in an ownership or managerial position in the league, as well?

ADAM SILVER: No, there have been no decisions about other members of the Sterling family, and I should say that this ruling applies specifically to Donald Sterling and Donald Sterling's conduct only.

Q. As you mentioned, over a dozen sponsors have dropped the Clippers. What has been the financial impact on this franchise and on the league from this scandal?

ADAM SILVER: I don't know. This has all happened in three days, and so I'm hopeful that there will be no long term damage to the league and to the Clippers' organization. But as I said earlier, I'm outraged, so I certainly understand other people's outrage, and it will take some time this will take some time, and appropriate healing will be necessary. I can understand precisely why, whether they be people affiliated with the NBA or the Clippers for a long time or those corporate partners. I can understand how upset they are, and I'll do my best to bring them back into the NBA family.

Q. If the owners vote three fourths vote not to force the sale, can you still under your powers institute the lifetime ban?

AADAM SILVER: The lifetime ban has been instituted. That is independent of forcing a sale of the team.

Q. Can you share with us what your initial reaction was when you first heard the voice on the tape and what it was espousing?

ADAM SILVER: When I first heard it, I was shocked. I was hoping somehow that it was fraudulent or that it had been doctored, that possibly it wasn't indeed Donald Sterling. I've known Donald for over 20 years, so I suspected it was his voice, and we set about immediately investigating, and that was my reaction, to sort of bear down and say let's get to the bottom of this as quickly as possible.

Q. Mayor Johnson has indicated he would like the league to undertake a full accounting of Donald Sterling's past and the failures by the NBA to act until now. Is that an account you'd be willing to undertake? And would you make any effort to mete out the personal views of other NBA owners at this point?

ADAM SILVER: I've had, as I said earlier, multiple conversations with Kevin Johnson, and I'm hoping that the actions we take today will satisfy our players. I believe they should.

Q. Can you just tell us, you said you've known Donald Sterling for 20 years. What have your interactions over those 20 years been like with him? Have you ever seen anything like this? Have you ever felt anything like this? And what kind of man did you judge him to be prior to this?

ADAM SILVER: I have not been that close to him over the years, but there's nothing I've ever seen in his behavior that would evidence these kinds of views. I've certainly, again, because there have been a lot of public filings about his activities, I've been aware of those accusations, but there's nothing I've ever seen firsthand that would indicate that he held the views that were expressed on these audio recordings.

Q. I'm curious, you spoke about your personal response to this. In terms of Donald Sterling self identifying as Jewish and you doing the same, as well, I'm wondering whether there was a specific kind of pain associated with that for you and if you felt a certain responsibility within the Jewish community to be responding to this in this way?

ADAM SILVER: I think my response was as a human being, and I used the word distraught before. I spoke on Saturday morning directly to Chris Paul, to Doc Rivers, and it wasn't even anger at that point. I mean, there was a certain somberness, and frankly, I felt sort of most strongly and personally for that team. While this affects every player and anyone associated with the NBA family, for those players and those coaches to go out and do what they need to do and play at the highest level in the world and have them hanging over this I think caused me to have a certain sadness I would say about the entire situation. I think this is regardless of anyone's religion, ethnicity, nationality. I think this is incredibly hurtful.

Q. At any time during your conversation with Mr. Sterling, did he express any remorse or denial regarding these comments?

ADAM SILVER: Mr. Sterling has not expressed those views directly to me.

Q. It's been suggested that the Clipper players be granted free agency at the end of this year as a result of this issue. Is that something that can be considered?

ADAM SILVER: That is not something we are considering.

Q. If you don't get the three quarter vote that you need, is it possible that Donald Sterling could still be an absentee owner profiting from this team even though physically he's banned from doing anything with it?

ADAM SILVER: I fully expect to get the support I need from the other NBA owners to remove him.

SUGGESTED READING

Jason Whitlock: *Culture Clash: Removing Sterling will not fix the systemic racism that gave birth to his attitudes*

See: espn.go.com/nba/story/_/id/10857268/ removing-donald-sterling-la-clippers-owner-fix-our-culture

Michael McCann: *Sterling, NBA set for epic legal fight over Clippers*

See: sportsillustrated.cnn.com/nba/news/20140429/ donald-sterling-nba-adam-silver-clippers-lawsuit-lifetime-ban/

Darren Heitner: *Should NBA Constitution Prevent Forced Sale Of Donald Sterling's Los Angeles Clippers?*

See: forbes.com/sites/darrenheitner/2014/04/30/ should-nba-constitution-prevent-forced-sale-of-donald-sterlings-los-angeles-clippers/

Dennis Prager: *What Have You Said in Private?*

See: dennisprager.com/said-private/

Kareem Abdul-Jabbar: Welcome to the Finger-Wagging Olympics

See: time.com/79590/ donald-sterling-kareem-abdul-jabbar-racism/

Emily Canal: *FORBES First Article On Donald Sterling Shows He Was A Loud Mouth Even Back Then*

Jason Whitlock: *Culture Clash: Removing Sterling will not fix the systemic racism that gave birth to his attitudes*

See: espn.go.com/nba/story/_/id/10857268/ removing-donald-sterling-la-clippers-owner-fix-our-culture

Michael McCann: *Sterling, NBA set for epic legal fight over Clippers*

See: sportsillustrated.cnn.com/nba/news/20140429/ donald-sterling-nba-adam-silver-clippers-lawsuit-lifetime-ban/

Darren Heitner: *Should NBA Constitution Prevent Forced Sale Of Donald Sterling's Los Angeles Clippers?*

See: forbes.com/sites/darrenheitner/2014/04/30/ should-nba-constitution-prevent-forced-sale-of-donald-ster-lings-los-angeles-clippers/

Dennis Prager: *What Have You Said in Private?*

See: dennisprager.com/said-private/

Kareem Abdul-Jabbar: Welcome to the Finger-Wagging Olympics

See: time.com/79590/ donald-sterling-kareem-abdul-jabbar-racism/

Emily Canal: *FORBES First Article On Donald Sterling Shows He Was A Loud Mouth Even Back Then*

See: forbes.com/sites/emilycanal/2014/05/15/ forbes-first-articles-on-donald-sterling-shows-he-was-a-loud-mouth-even-back-then/

Hua Hsu and Richard Jean So: *Donald Sterling's Model Minority: What the Clippers owner's love of Koreans reveals about racism in America.*

See:slate.com/articles/sports/sports_nut/2014/05/donald_sterling_koreans_what_the_clippers_owner_s_love_of_korean_americans.html

Twitchy Staff: *'End of 'free speech' in America'? Joyce Carol Oates reflects on Sterling lifetime ban*

See: twitchy.com/2014/04/30/end-of-free-speech-in-america-joyce-carol-oates-reflects-on-sterling-lifetime-ban/

PROLOGUE:

How A Cocky Kid From Philly Turned A Once Die-Hard Pistons Fan Into A Lakers Fan And Bought Him A House To Boot

It was the summer of 1996 and I was seventeen years old. Basketball had been my first love for many years. I had skipped countless days of school to play pickup games at the local park, walked home from school upon learning that my favorite college team was playing an afternoon NCAA tournament game, and even skipped out on my second and third loves (video games and food) in order to play up to 10 hours a day that summer.

I had become quite good at the game I loved, perhaps not NBA level good but quite possibly good enough to earn a living playing professionally in an overseas league. I was a 6'2" (read 6'4" in NBA terms) combo guard who could pass the rock beautifully and rebound like a player 6" taller. I also had an incredibly diverse offensive repertoire that featured an adept post game and deadly range and accuracy on my jumper (I loved taking bets from jokers who didn't think I could hit insanely deep 3's on the playground). I still remember the first time I was ever asked for an autograph - I was 12 years old and had just finished scoring every single point for my team, including many extremely deep three-pointers (for those of you who remember the University of Arkansas Razorbacks' Alex Dillard, you get the idea) during a streetball tournament game victory. I felt as if the world was mine that day and Stacey Augmon himself couldn't have stopped me (unless of course Richard Perry paid him to let me score, ahem, ahem).

Of course I was also a loose cannon that never got along with my coaches, talked a great deal of trash to opposing players, berated my own teammates for doing anything other than passing me the ball and stopped playing anything but street tournaments and blacktop games of 1-on-1 and the like long before I graduated from high school. In short, I was a prototypical knucklehead.

I had visions of *walking* on at the University of Nevada Las Vegas (UNLV) and while that may not have been entirely realistic (though I do believe I could have made their 1997-98 squad as a freshman and played behind New Zealand's Mark Dickel - who could really ball by the way), I have no real doubt that I could have played Division One ball *somewhere*. Alas, playing college ball was not meant to be, and thank God for that! Instead I fell in love with the woman of my dreams, repented of my sins and gave my life to the Lord and Savior Jesus Christ of Nazareth, entered the ministry (though I now consider myself a Biblical Christian rather than any particular denomination as I am still not very fond of organized religion and would rather just serve my God, obey His word, and let the chips fall where they may), became a father of nine amazing children (at the time of this writing – who knows what the future holds) and all but gave up on actually playing the game I once loved so dearly.

There was also the matter of an irregular heart-beat, flipping out of a construction truck and landing on my back, messing up both my ankles and knees as well as my back and even later not being able to walk for quite a while due to a slipped disc in my back, but honestly all of that is beside the point. God became my first love and basketball, well, basketball is still is the *game* I love more than any other!

Enough about me and my not so illustrious hoops credentials - back to the summer of 1996. That summer was a great time to be alive, a great time to be a basketball fan and an even greater time to be a Laker fan, for that summer a new NBA dynasty was created, thanks in large part to *The Logo*, Jerry West. During the summer of 96' West pulled off perhaps the single most lop sided and some would say clairvoyant trade in the history of the NBA when he convinced the Charlotte Bobcats to trade the rights to the 13th pick in the NBA Draft (a pick the Lakers used on 17 year old Kobe Bean Bryant) for Serbian center Vlade Divac.

While many people excuse the Hornets titanic blunder, believing there was no way they could have known a mere high school kid would turn out to be the second coming of Michael Jordan and one of the three best scorers (along with Jordan and the great Wilt Chamberlain) to ever step foot on a basketball court, such isn't exactly true. The truth is that Kobe Bryant was the son of former superstar collegian and very solid NBA player Joe Bryant (who averaged 21.8 points per game and 11.4 rebounds per game on .517 shooting in his final collegiate season at LaSalle), nephew of former NBA player Chubby Cox (who was drafted by the Chicago Bulls in 1978 and last played for the Washington Bullets during the 1982-83 season - and yes that really was what his friend's called him though his birth name was John Arthur Cox III), had just finished leading a once moribund high school program (Lower Merion High School) to a state title, and even crushed the aforementioned Wilt Chamberlain's Pennsylvania high school career scoring record of 2,252 points by scoring an obscene 2,883 points. The kid known as Bean had even been named both the *Naismith High School Player of the Year* and the *Gatorade Men's National Basketball Player of the Year.*

Bryant was also known to have destroyed one of the NCAA's top scorers in pre-draft work-outs, a 6'8, 220 lb. small forward and grown man by the name of Dontae Jones. Jones had just finished leading the Mississippi State Bulldogs to an SEC tournament championship (which he earned MVP honors of) and an unexpected Final Four berth after being named the Regional MVP along the way. Clearly Kobe Bean Bryant was something special.

Of course, it's also true that Vlade Divac was no slouch. Divac was known as perhaps the best passing center in the league as well as one of the best passing centers of all-time. When it became common knowledge that the Hornets had never even considered drafting Bryant before trading the rights to the pick to the Lakers, it became obvious that trading for Vlade Divac was far better than drafting one of the available center prospects in the 1996 Draft such as Efthimios Rentzias or Priest Lauderdale. However, no matter how one spins it, the Bryant for Divac trade will live in infamy and may even be regarded as the beginning of *the Kobe curse* for as long as the Hornets remain a basketball team, be they in Charlotte, New Orleans, or China one day (though if they moved to China they could be called the *Dragons,* have a great mascot and serve the best sushi of any NBA team, and that alone would be cause for celebration).

Less than one month after acquiring Bryant, Jerry West would pull off the impossible and convince the most dominant physical force the game had ever seen, Shaquille O'Neal, to leave *Disney World* and the Orlando Magic for *Disney Land* and the greatest franchise in professional sports. The Los Angeles Lakers were back, *Showtime* was back and I was pumped!

Shaquille O'Neal had been my favorite player since the first time I watched him play a game at Louisiana State University. While most kids my age, and for that matter adults my size, seemed to gravitate to the guards and perhaps wing players, there was just something about the *Shaq Attack* that I found especially awesome. Although I was a natural guard who loved to shoot deep threes, I began working on my post-up game relentlessly and the first time someone called me *baby Shaq* during a pickup game I was elated.

As Shaq was my favorite player the Orlando Magic instantly became my favorite team in the summer of 92', supplanting my beloved Detroit Pistons, a team I had grown up rooting for and had season tickets to with my mother during their *Bad Boys* years. However when Shaq was drafted by the Magic, I was a Magic man through and through.

The above said, it goes without saying that when Shaq signed with the Lakers, the Lakers would instantly become my favorite team, a near sports-blasphemy for a one-time die-hard Pistons fan. However, truth be told there was something about that cocky, smiling kid from Philly that had been drafted less than a month earlier that had already had me leaning towards becoming a die-hard Lakers fan.

Over the course of the 1996-97 season something strange happened to me. Shaquille O'Neal, the great *Shaq Attack* that had been my favorite player for around seven years had become my second favorite player. The cocky, smiling kid from Philly had won my basketball heart.

Over the next six years I read just about everything I could about Kobe Bryant and quickly felt that while I had never met him we were somehow kindred spirits. I had never felt that way about Shaq, I had simply been amazed by his power and attracted to his personality but with Kobe I literally felt as if I had a personal connection, and honestly there were some interesting similarities. Kobe and I were nearly the same age, we were both thought to be extremely intelligent but also hard-headed, we each married a woman, and at an age, that our family didn't necessarily agree with, we each had a falling out with our family that wasn't caused by any overt fault of our own, we each had a me-against-the-world mentality (I used to start my days listening to *F**k the World* by 2PAC – which honestly, even as a Christian I can still appreciate a great deal, as to be a Christian is to be in the world but not of it and therefore to have a *me-against-the-world* mentality), and of course, we were both Laker fans!

There was also a financial connection between Kobe Bryant and I, as strange as that may sound. You see, I was raised by a mother who was very wise with her money, a father who despised working for anyone but himself and a Grandmother who not only lavished me with copious financial gifts (such as giving me $250 for receiving an A on my report card when most of my friends might receive $5-10 for such, or $500 in bribe money to assure that I wouldn't play high school football when the only way my friends could make $500 was to work full-time for two weeks in the summer) but encouraged me to invest and increase the funds I was given rather than spend them on video games or clothes like most of my school age buddies did. All of this combined to make me, what I like to refer as, a *self-employed wise gambler,* and yes I know the term wise gambler sounds like an oxymoron but I was indeed a gambler and I was no moron.

I had always been interested in sports cards and sports memorabilia growing up and at one time I had some of the nicest and most valuable Shaquille O'Neal, Marshall Faulk and Drew Bledsoe collections on the planet. When Kobe Bryant came on the scene in 1996 I literally felt like I had to invest in him, just had too.

I decided to sell just about every single card and autographed jersey, ball and picture I had in my collection and use those funds, along with those I received from selling *Disney* stock and my own personal savings ($250 per A adds up pretty quick) to purchase as many Kobe Bryant *Topps Finest* rookie cards as I could get my hands on. Back then eBay wasn't very big and I had to go to local card shows almost every weekend to stock up; however after a while I had quite a stack of the gorgeous shiny bronze cards with funny peel attached called *Topps Finest*.

Had I merely held onto this stack of cards until after the Lakers 3-peat in 2002 I certainly could have turned a huge profit, however I was far too much of a gambler to just sit on such an investment. Instead I started researching ways to multiply the value of my new collection, be it through trading the cards for autographed items or even sending the cards themselves to Kobe through the mail to get autographed (generally not a good idea unless the cards you are sending are *commons* and not of significant value, or unless you enjoy losing cards, though I will say that when I wrote to Shaquille O'Neal and Tracy McGrady at one point, each player did send me an autographed item through the mail). However, what I decided to do turned out to be the best decision possible in my estimation. I had found out that the *Topps Chrome* rookie cards of Kobe, which at that time were far less valuable than the *Topps Finest* version I had a pile of, were in fact far rarer. Knowing that supply and demand is the primary factor in escalating values for items I decided straight away to trade all of my *Topps Finest* Kobe rookie cards for as many *Topps Chrome* Kobe rookie cards as I could get my hands on - and boy oh boy was I successful in doing so!

When the dust settled and I had a massive stack of the *Topps Chrome* rookie cards, which by this time were extremely coveted and selling for many times what the *Topps Finest* rookie cards were selling for, I decided that owning a home would be far more worthwhile than owning a stack of cardboard pieces with pictures on them, even if those pieces of cardboard were chrome colored and shiny and the pictures were of Kobe Bryant. Thanks to the good Lord I was able to sell that stack of sports cards and purchase my first home with my precious wife, with nothing but good ole cash money! Today I can literally and honestly say with a smile that Kobe Bryant, at least in part, bought me my first house.

INTRODUCTION

I have always been a jock but perhaps even more so a stats-geek and money-man. Ever since I was extremely young I have been a bit of a walking calculator, able to do many mathematical equations in my head faster than another can do with a calculator at his or her disposal. When I became interested in sports, it was only natural that I would instantly also become interested in player's salaries, team salary constraints and the like.

After I basically hung up my high-tops for good in order to give my ankles, knees and back a break, the financial side of the game invaded my mind even more. When websites like RealGM.com and HoopsHype.com with its team salary pages came on-line, I was in arm-chair GM heaven. I quickly memorized the salaries of perhaps over 100 players and began constructing trades in my head and on-paper to improve every team in the league. I also started writing on various websites and forums which almost always led to my being kicked off the site by some overzealous moderator or cyber-Nazi who happened to disagree with my opinions on his or her favorite team's problems and how to fix them with a trade that made both basketball and financial sense. Such is life.

No matter, when the urge to write a trade proposal crept up I simply searched the web for another website, and of course, used a separate pseudonym. I even ran my own sports blog for a short time until I realized that I just didn't have enough time to dedicate to it, with all the other family, ministry and writing projects I was involved in. However when the 2012-13 season ended, I was a bit burned out. Life was happening, our ninth child was on the way, my family and I were planning a cross country relocation and I simply disappeared from the forums and websites I had once so passionately haunted.

Life is still happening and now just eight months after relocating and getting all settled in we are once again in an entirely different locale (after yet another long and strenuous relocation), this time settling into a recently purchased home we would like to actually live in for more than 12 months.

However, although life is still as unpredictable as ever, the 2013-14 NBA season is almost finished, the Boston Celtics are an enigma after trading franchise savior's Paul Pierce and Kevin Garnett and signing a coach who looks like he could be playing ball on my 14 year old son's team in Brad Stevens (a great hire in my mind by the way), and, most importantly, the Celtics have the pieces necessary (expiring contracts, cap space, draft picks and talented tradeable players) to build an NBA championship level roster in short order. At a time like this, how could I not write about the Celtics?

As for where the idea for a Be the General Manager and Choose your Own Ending Sports Adventure book came from, such is an easy question to answer. My children and even I myself have always enjoyed Choose Your

Own Adventure books and I have been the quintessential arm-chair General Manager for years now; simply put, I was bound to write a book like this someday. And, with the Celtics having the necessary pieces to recreate their entire team and turn one of the worst teams in 2013-14 into one of the best teams in 2014-15 I thought now was the perfect time to write this book. Of course, it also made perfect sense to write this book after having recently finished Saving the Lakers: A Be the General Manager Book, so there's that too.

Anyways, my hope is that young and old Celtics fans, stat-geeks, number-crunchers, arm-chair GM's and just plain basketball fans alike will enjoy this book and read it again and again and again, until they make all the correct choices necessary to win the championship. The truth is that winning the title on one's first read-through of this book is much, much, much harder to do than winning the NBA title is for any player in the league today, period.

There are only 30 teams in the league which means that every team starts the season with a 1-in-30 chance of winning the title or 30/1 odds. However, in order to win the championship in this book, you will have to beat incredible odds. How incredible you ask? Simply put, you literally have a better chance of actually playing in the NBA than you have of winning the title on your first read-through of this book; yes, I'm serious!

The odds that you win the title on your first read through of this book are exactly 995,330 / 1. That's right nine- hundred and ninty-five thousand, three-hundred and thirty to one! You literally have a .00000100469 percent chance of winning the title on your first read through of this book!

Simply put, there are about 80 countries on the face of planet earth whose entire populations could read and try to win the title on their first read through of this book without even one single citizen doing so. In the good ole U.S.A, if every single one of its 317,000,000 citizens, including the comatose, infants and Otis Smith, read this book, a whopping 318 people would be able to win the title on their first read-through. In comparison there are well over 500 players and coaches in the NBA today. Think about that. No seriously, really think about that; it's insane!

If you can conquer this book and win the title on your first, or even your tenth read-through, you could be a real life NBA General Manager one day. I honestly believe that, especially considering Otis Smith was once hired as a General Manager. All of that said, read carefully, chose wisely, stay true to who you are, make the decisions you feel will help the team win the 2014-15 NBA title … and don't forget to have fun!

Notes

Notes

ABOUT THE AUTHOR

Bryant T. Jordan is the author of *Saving the Lakers: A Be the General Manager Book* and *Saving the Celtics: A Be the General Manager Book.* He has been a freelance writer for over 15 years.

BTJ as many know him lives in a rural paradise with his high-school sweetheart and wife of 17 plus years, as well as his magnificent children, under the amazing care of His God and Savior. He considers himself the most blessed man on the planet, period.

You can generally find him leaving thought-proving tweets on Twitter @bryantTjordan

www.BryantTJordan.com